THE SEARCH

FOR

ADELE PARKER

To Rob and Lisa
who would have adored her

THE SEARCH

FOR

ADELE PARKER

by

Robert Charlton Hull

Library of Congress Catalog No. 74-82751

Copyright 1974 by Libra Publishers, Inc.
391 Willets Road
Roslyn Heights, N.Y. 11577

Manufactured in the United States of America

This is a memory book.

It is how a great number of people remember Adele Parker. Conceivably, it is not all true but is largely true—the kinds of things people keep with them and pass on, and, when all is said and done, grow from.

Most of all, it is the warmth and the humor and the good of the place they once called Parker's Ranch.

". . . You will do well to go out today and say goodbye to gallant old Bill Cody and his gallant crew. Take the kids for conscience sake. And tell them to remember what they see."

—Arthur Greene
Morning Oregonian
September 26, 1908

TABLE OF CONTENTS

ACKNOWLEDGMENTS

Thanks are extended to Miss Mary Rankin, confidant and associate of Adele Parker, who graciously provided the author with Mrs. Parker's journals and daybooks from 1949 to her death in 1966; also to Eugenia Ellis and Jean Tomer, co-associates of Parker's Ranch, who likewise shared and lived that unreal world; to Dolly Bateman, Mrs. Parker's cousin, for her helpfulness.

To Thomas R. Vickery for his special permission to use material from his two Parker tributes, "Sketches From The Life Of a Grande Dame," 1955, and "The Walnut Trees," 1966; to North Olmsted police chief George Christman and to police lieutenant Clifford Biddulph for their invaluable accounts; to R.I Frost, curator of the Buffalo Bill Museum in Cody, Wyoming, for permission to re-photograph early pictures of Mrs. Parker's Wild West days; to Dorothy Fyfe, Mrs. Parker's childhood neighbor, who took the author on a pilgrimage to Adele's Plainfield, New Jersey homestead.

To horse trainer and showman Robert Gump, whose expressive humor, insight and candor compelled the completion of this book; to Fred Garlow, grandson of Buffalo Bill, whose recollection of Adele remains crisp and distinct; to circus man Harry Hollins who remembers Mrs. Parker in the center ring; to Harris M. Richard of the Plainfield Public Library and to W. Gale Hoffman, president of The Historical Society of Plainfield and North Plainfield, New Jersey, for their efforts in tracing the von Ohl family; to showman Orilla Downing Hollister for her descriptions of Adele and the 1908 Buffalo Bill Wild West tour, and for her insight into the personality of Colonel Cody; to the Parker neighbors, Jean and Jerry McKenna, to whom something "Parker's Ranchish" was perpetually occurring.

To Day Camp Counselor Peg Neneman; to the blacksmith Walter Page; to Cleveland Public Library and to Park County Library (Cody, Wyoming) for their splendid help in securing microfilms of accounts of the original Buffalo Bill shows; to former ranch veterinarians Cliff Wagner and Wallace Wendt for their professional commentary; to William

Townsend of the Cleveland Society for Crippled Children for his description of Mrs. Parker's efforts for that charity.

My thanks, as well, to the following special friends, riders, students, neighbors and passers-by who spent hours shinnying down memories of Parker's Ranch years: Ruth Angel, Carol Becker, Charlotte Barlik, A.Z. Baker, E. Christine Baker, Dr. and Mrs. Gerhard Berg, A.T. Burrows, Frances and Arthur Bibbs, Roberta Durey Bell, Dr. Richard Beargie, Edward and Portia Bergh, Dr. Sally Becker, Jean Carroll, William Phelps Corbett, Constance Clarin, Shirley Care, Carol Christianson, Mrs. Robert Cahoon and Lynn Cahoon, Mrs. Frank Cansky and Sharlyn Cansky, W.E. Cook, Dottie Correll, Robert A Charvat, Mrs. John F. Day, Ruth Douglas, Shirley Durey, A.E. Frantz, Mr. and Mrs. Charles Gentsch, Frieda Geiger, Mrs. Inga Grail, Karl Granger, Carole Durey Hall, F.L. Heltman, Mrs. James Hodgkiss, Lucile Hiserod, Shirley Harmon, Sharon Colwell Hetzel, Larry Harold, Marty Harayda, Russ and Curly Janus, Edward Josham, Barbara Ewig Jaquays, Helen Kolleda, Peggy Knight, Mrs. Rose Kloos, Ernest Kinzer, Cindy Kouris, Sally Wagner Knurek, Marie Kresge, Miriam Worth Ketchem, Jackie Loehr Kaesgen, Phyllis Krueger, I.H. Lorom, Mary Alice Lynch, Hulda and Greta Lesher, Mrs. Helen Lodwick, Dr. James Lemmon and Mrs. Lemmon, Judy Leibtag, Lynn Polatsek Martin, Kay and Tom Matowitz, Ray Metsch, Maribel Mullen Marabito, Mrs. Hope Matlak, Robert Neff, Mrs. John O'Stafy, Luther E. Paddoch, Marguerite Gormar Poley, Leann Kline Papp, Mrs. Judith Petro, Mrs. Clayton A. Quintrell, Mrs. E. Clyde Rosha, Mrs. John Rezzigi, Mrs. Carolyn Paisley Seelbach, Whitney Slaght, Jr., Mrs. Ruth Stewart, Karl Stats, Virda Stewart, Mrs. Vida Smith and Bonnie Smith, David Schmidtke, Paul W. Snearer, DLee Spathalf, Sue Smith, Florence Sutton, William Tessmann, Martha Gentsch Thomas, Harvey Turley, Paul Vick, Mrs. Linda Walker, Mrs. Lloyd S. Wallace, Sue Neneman Wendt, Mary Townes Waller, Mrs. Morton Wyman, Ann Wiktor, Carol Williamson, Alta Yeltz, Blanche Zerkowitz, Maria Zankowich

. . . and to all the Parker animals, wherever you are.

THE DISCUSSION

"You are a woman, a writer of respected reputation, and a prominent psychologist. Tell me, was Adele von Ohl Parker a *noble* woman? Give me a word that applies. . ."

"Concerned."

"Concerned. . . I believe I reject your choice. I think of a concerned person in a far different sense. I think of a person who is totally receptive and *caring* about my problems, and in me as a person. Not in who I might be but in who I am. Cognizant of my flaws, my difficulties. . ."

"Ah, she didn't care about your *difficulties*. . ."

"Thus, I reject the word 'concern.' "

"The difference is the way we're looking at the word. You're looking at *concern* as *you* would feel it. I'm looking at concern as the feeling Adele had. And Adele and you and I are three different persons. Adele was concerned with things as they applied to her or rather as she applied to them. She looked at things only on a one-to-one basis—always! Adele and this. Adele and that. What she felt was truly concern. But it wasn't your concern, or mine—it was Adele's. And what I admired so was the incredible strength."

"A teen-ager in braids hoped the book would be called *The Search For Adele Parker*."

"An interesting theme—yes. . . because of course *she* was searching for Adele Parker, too. . ."

"Really? But she appeared so positive, so cock-sure, so loudly, flashingly demonstrative that people would say, 'THERE'S a person who knows who she is and what she wants!"

"No. No. There were too many weak spots. She was never sure. . . First, she was completely illogical, which is to say completely paradoxical. Well, look for yourself. One picture of Adele—a woman with so much disrespect for soft females. *Incredible* disrespect. Yet so concerned with 'ladylike' behavior. This was entirely paradoxical."

"And respect for parents?"

"Yes, to the point of phobia. Respect for age was another thing she so often spoke of. Yet she had no respect for her sister's age. She spoke many things that she didn't live. Yet you felt when she said them that she meant them intensely. When she didn't live them, it wasn't because she was living opposite to her belief but because it was the only way she had to adjust, and sometimes, it is adjust or die."

"Many thousands knew her first as a child. At what point would one first be apt to feel doubt in this woman?"

"I suppose when you found out she could make a mistake. And you would *have* to decide, ultimately, that she had definitely made some mistakes, or she wouldn't be in such a mess. She did give the kids the impression she was God. And when they found out she wasn't, it must have been rather hard."

"What was lacking? What was her flaw?"

"Reality."

"At what age might one suspect that there were things even more important in the world than those she spoke of all her life?"

"Most *never* suspected because they lost contact with her. They would have to have grown and gone through school and married and had a child or two. And then taken a look and said, 'Boy, that place has changed!' And of course it HADN'T! *They* had changed. And of course the ones who didn't change—who continued to go there, and live there, who became one with Parker's Ranch—were infused in the dream."

PROLOGUE
by Thomas Vickery

I got a sulky letter from somebody I rented a limousine from in November, 1965. It was a station wagon, actually, but a driver came with it in a hat to wait out the Horse Show at Madison Square Garden and opened the door and my lawyer asked me when I told him about the letter, if I was broke that month how could I rent station wagons and I told him it was for a woman and left him holding his head.

The circumstance was a gift making up the last days of a romance that has occupied thirty years of my life which only leaves six unaccounted for. This kind of love affair even my lawyer can't take lightly and so I'm going to send him this and maybe he will return the letter from the car people and I'll have something else to look at and remember.

It all started when I was six, back in Cleveland, and a horse tried to run over me. The next time I saw a horse I tried to run up a wall and somebody told my mother where people could go to forget about this kind of fear, young or old, which was about the best advice we ever got from anybody.

It was called Parker's Ranch, run by Adele von Ohl Parker, who had come to town in 1929 to perform at Keith's Palace Theater with her horses and found the Depression had blown the Palace doors shut along with Vaudeville in general. While the world around her got busy liquidating, she built a riding hall out of an abandoned stockyard, put the neighborhood kids to work running it, found more horses, started a polo team, and finally moved the whole thing (with the help of half the town) out to a place hung on the.rim of the Metropolitan Park over a stream now known as Parker's Creek.

"Something of a gypsy, this Mrs. Parker!" the people said. Something of a grande dame; compelling, wild, beautiful, frightening, well—my God! How can anybody today describe it. And her dying somewhere around eighty or eighty-five doesn't help describe it because dying was never any problem for her, only for the rest of us kicking around without the same equipment for living she had.

And all of us, the three or four or five thousand who got busted, kissed, taught or touched by her and fell in love tried to forestall that event, fighting it all those years, which gave us more in common than most people ever have.

Just about everybody was heard from the week she died.

She came out to Brookville to see us the previous November. She got on a bus near Parker's Ranch and rode all night and went to the Garden Show all day and waited for me in the evening performance, looking smaller than I remembered, and after the performance we came out in this "elegant" station wagon and she said some things to the driver coming out that got him carrying her bags into the house and upstairs and hanging around until he ran out of excuses.

If it had been her house she would have asked him to stay the night.

But what I'm trying to get across to my lawyer and these car people is what happened when I was six. I don't really remember being afraid of horses; somehow she managed that the first week. I got told about being afraid much later. Adele Parker is a complete history that started in Plainfield, New Jersey; a very pretty little girl in a paper tu tu trying to ride standing bareback on a pony after she spread walnuts around the ring to discourage falling off. Also showing, hunting, driving, winning.

"The Walnut Trees" is another thing I have, sketched here that November, because of that story.

Then all those incredible years like 1905 jumping horses from a tower into a tank of water at the Hippodrome, jumping astride at Atlantic City, all that ungovernable, joyous, intractable doing. The Ringling Bros. Circus around 1919, and Barnum and Bailey, working these horses off the hind legs, working to the people; always the unexpected.

The movies and the people. Life with Tom Mix, Will Rogers, George Ringling and Buffalo Bill Cody.

"The pick up," she said once. "With the Cody show we used to bet people a fifty dollar gold piece. Here, the rider swings down at full gallop to pick the gold piece off the ground in his teeth. That was easy," she said, "it was the Indians who gave me trouble. One act was melee where I got captured, pulled down from the horses. They were real Indians, you know. Sometimes they forgot it was just a show."

Who has these stories? The scars and healed over breaks and wild horse hunts and the children, this legion of us who had listened and really lived like Indians and circus people and trick riders and tough hombres on her horses, in her barns, through her woods, and the whole incomprehensible, irreplaceable fabric of life she generated.

The elephants. Oh, Jesus! Remember the elephants; the time an old circus friend, broke, with nothing left but his elephants, came out to Parker's Ranch? And we had real elephants to ride and went down into the valley, swimming the elephants in the river and they ate her out of hay and the Park Commissioner came up screaming about crazy calls he got that there were elephants in his park. What kid had elephants to ride when he was six or sixteen?

Gene Autry came once. The real Gene Autry. And the whole side pasture where the elephants had been was full of his horses and the whole front pasture was full of Champion and I slept out there wrapped up in a horse blanket next to the fence. I woke up with the dew on me and Champion right there and never knew she had spent two hours looking for me in the night and that when she found me she didn't do anything. She just looked at me and went back to the house.

And when you were seventeen and fit and so slap dash almighty man and horseman in the evening playing capture the flag she came bustling out of the woods on the George Hanover horse of hers and down you went off your animal, kicking in the shale along the river, wondering what hit you and how you lost the flag.

Who has these stories?

And so in November, 1965, we sat down by our Brookville paddock while she sketched the walnut trees and watched the kids ride two horses we have which upsets my lawyer also, and the stories came on that strong voice.

"You need some more fence," she said, "to make it safer

for the kids. I'm going to give you a fence."

Who gives anybody a fence? Who would think of it? Somebody like that with all those years and seventy horses, six dogs and many cats, chickens and ducks, who was once billed the highest paid actress in New York and has three or four or five thousand long-term love affairs going.

Somebody alive with life.

Later we went to see Anna Marie Thinnes' Andalusian horses at Bailey's place. Mrs. Parker had on a dress and wool bermuda socks and couldn't keep off the horses and rode them part of the afternoon. In her skirt, the whole rig out, she was something to see. You didn't notice anything. You just kept watching the way she rode a horse. When she climbed on Gallardo she carried all this grace and the horse just picked it up and they worked it out together.

She never disappointed anyone. You couldn't oversell her at any distance.

The next day we found her some coveralls and she rode again; we bought two of the Spanish saddles because they fit all the wounds. She was just filled with it; making plans for the riding she could do in those saddles.

"Everything I ever wished for," she said, "everything has come true. Just when I was feeling a little tired in the joints. Now these saddles. I don't know anything about God except that He's been awful busy taking care of me.

"You know, Vickery," she said, the way she does, using your last name when she's going to come down on you, "I like the way you sit a horse but I wish you'd get the ends of your reins on the right side of his neck."

We put her on the bus at midnight with another one of her kids, a young lady who is riding jumping horses for the Mexican Army and calls her Madam.

She went away on the bus with the two saddles wrapped in burlap sacks and she's gone and I'm here with the "Walnut Trees, November, 1965" and maybe if my lawyer understands any of this, I'll get that letter back from the car people.

Adele von Ohl Parker

CHAPTER 1

A LOT OF THINGS THAT DON'T HAPPEN ANYMORE

"Sometimes the pines, down the hill and across Parker's Creek, roar," old Vickery wrote in that soft, mewing way of his. "It is hard to explain it any other way. When they do that, it generally snows. The coons are night-running then, beating small paths across the bank. They stop and listen at the stamp of a horse's foot or at the uneasy song of the wind in the giant oak by the water trough. It is a familiar patch of earth to them. Under the looming shadow of the barns, they have raised unmolested generations in easy comraderie with the ranch people. . ."

Tom Vickery often wrote and dreamed of Parker's Ranch, that patch of unique fairyland of our childhood in North Olmsted, Ohio, and of its vigorous, ingenious, utopian mistress, Adele von Ohl Parker.

No worshiper, I, but you can go anywhere—to Maine, New York, Kentucky, Michigan—*no matter!*—*Somebody* has known her and has had happy experiences. We were driving down the New York Throughway and a truck driver in a van came zinging by, flashing his lights. He pulled over and said, "I seen the decal 'Parker's Ranch' on y'r bumper. *How is she? Is she still awright?* I learned to ride there as a little kid!"

Parker with the valley wind in her hair. . . Mrs. Parker around the campfire. . . what of Mrs. Parker the person? What was she? *Who* was she? Thousands will tell you, "I knew Mrs. Parker!" And they may only have said hello. She made you feel you knew her *intimately.* She could float through hospitals (which she often did) and perk up six dozen patients at a crack. She had a warmth, a vibrance about her—but that was *about* her. . .

Was that Mrs. Parker or wasn't it? What Mary, her dear friend, is saying about those who use that much damned expression, "good old Ma Parker," making *believe* they knew her. . . they thought they *did* know her! And she would lead them to believe they did. People don't call everyone "ma" or "mother." She even professed, on numerous occasions, that they were *all* her children.

But let something occur to contemplate your leaving. You might as well tell her you were going to burn Jesus off the Cross, you could be no more of a sinner.

"HOW CAN YOU DO THIS TO ME! IF YOU GO DOWN THAT DRIVE, DON'T *EVER* COME BACK!"

Pleading one minute, threatening the next—she would turn tears and rage on and off like a switch. It not only proved effective, it was convenient. One reporter called her "Ethel Barrymore in spurs." No one forgot that. Never.

Indeed, Parker's Ranch became symbolic of a lot of things that don't happen anymore. Adele spun its atmosphere with a particular regard to simplicity. Like anything essentially simple, the ranch was full of surprises and contradictions.

The essential one was Mrs. Parker, herself.

At Parker's Ranch if you wished to talk about a cow, you could find somebody to talk about a cow. If you desired to philosophize or tackle oriental religion, you could uncover a philosopher or discommode a theologian. If your interest was the morals of a burlesque house, you could find someone to rise to that.

But you accepted things as you found them or you didn't go back. There were inevitable surprises. You never asked who someone was, why he was there, where he came from, where he went? No, never.

A person was simply there or no longer there. All part of the grand, continuing and everlasting quality of mystery of the place.

I can remember Adele Parker sitting on the back porch with a bottle of goat's milk in two parts, water and curd. She would put an egg in it or she would offer flax seed tea, which was nothing but one long string. Parents would hear of this and prescribe a good vomit, a bowel movement and a bath.

The impression of so many upon arriving down that long, dusty drive was that they were sure as hell in the wrong place, and that they better get out fast before they got bit by something or caught a disease!

Nobody could mistake Adele Parker if they saw her. Even

2

if one had never seen her before, you knew from what others had told you. Her complexion was tanned, the skin rough, leathery. To the end she had all her teeth and a Stetson hundred-gallon hat. Except in pictures she showed me, I never saw her hair down. Always in some kind of twist—a French twist—or on top of her head in a bun or roll; in pigtails in her youth. . .

Her expressions made her face. In anger she had a deceptively hard face. When happy (which was most of the time), she was beautiful.

Her youngsters still speak of her variety of hats. There was the green tam, the Stetson tied up with a scarf, a Mexican hat. She went in fits and starts. By her hats, one could predict her mood with prophetic accuracy. When she came out, slamming the door, wearing the tam hautily cocked on the side of her head, everybody ran. We knew very well we were in for it. She wore that green tam before all wild west shows. It was like Samson's hair. It provided that extra bite.

A kid once asked about the strange little outbuilding in the back, "Did you ever look in there and see Mrs. Parker's show clothes hanging like a corpse?"

Indeed, her hat hung from the ceiling, her jacket, skirt and boots directly beneath so that it appeared a whole person. That little house—that little octagonal thing—was reserved for her show clothes. That's where they hung. Sure enough, every time you passed by it, you had a queasy feeling as though she were standing inside looking out.

Clothes in general meant nothing to her. Once, when a neighbor stopped to transport her to the opera, Adele had completely forgotten and had nothing to wear. "Be right with you, though!" she chirped. Pulling down a drape and wrapping it about herself like a shroud, she stuck in a few pins and threw up her hair—and looked like a queen!

Mrs. Parker would motor off without a thought or a suitcase. "Why bother with clothes and things!" she'd laugh. "I'll find some somewhere. *Something* will happen!" It did. It did for her. It happened only for her.

We saw her usually in a pair of trousers, often in frontier pants and a pretty shirt and nice hat—then she was dressed

3

up, but to see her in a dress was unusual—like the black suit, the black velvet suit she came to the voting booth in. Then if the horse needed shoes, she'd tackle the job, dress and all. You could not be sure what she would do.

She was an inquisitive person. If a horse became ill or injured and had to be "put down," she performed her own autopsies. "I saw one of them," commented Dr. Richard Beargie, a successful eye surgeon in Lakewood, Ohio, "I'll never forget it. I can still see her plain as day carving up this animal, tracking down its lingering ailment. She would ask me innumerable questions as she carved and probed. But I could not look at it though I was a quarter of the way to becoming a surgeon."

Near the third barn was a summer house and an incredible pasture. It wasn't unusual to wander back and find a pony troop camped there for weeks. Elks Circus once had elephants chained in this pasture. She let the children ride them and take them down the trail and water them in a secret pond in a place called Paradise.

A policeman I know laughs when he remembers her. But not a horse laugh.

"A horde of kids would have simply cluttered the streets if it hadn't been for that character," he chuckled gently. "Many didn't have money to ride, yet spent the whole day there. Parker's Ranch didn't profit by it. Parker tolerated it. Some would get their 50¢ together and would ride a little while and that's all they'd spend in a week but they'd be there half the summer."

There were so *many people's* footprints in those fifteen acres of different world. The fat, the simple, the ugly, the troubled... persons going through divorces... alcoholics... all found a ready-made haven.

"My father worried when I lived there at ten years of age," whispered Sue Neneman Wendt, wife of the veterinarian, "that what I would want all my life would be to shovel manure and ride horses. The truth of it was, I didn't. Yet at Mrs. Parker's death, it was as if half my life suddenly had flown when I revisited the shell of a house and watched the barns burn. I had spent so much of my existence there. I owe my

4

husband to the ranch. I owe all of my compassion and affection for life to the ranch."

We found there more than a few discouraged-looking cats and odoriforous goats, yet it was a place for soul-searching. A place without interruptions or holocausts. For some it recalled "You Can't Take It With You." No counterfeit bill-making in the cellar. But you had real Indians, who, with a fair consistency, broke into Adele Parker's wine and threatened to burn down the whole world.

"You know," said a housewife, "how barns are usually so dirty? Mrs. Parker always said, 'People talk about dirty barns but they all have a purpose.' She'd tell us how cobwebs can be used to stop hemorrhaging of horses. Now I tell everyone when they complain about my house, 'You never can tell when a horse might canter past, bleeding to death!' "

The sons of an Elyria woman said to their mother in 1965, "For four years you've been raving about this Parker's Ranch and we finally decided we'd find out what it was. We went over there and none of us would *believe* it! What do you *see* in that place? All run down in the heels, it needs six coats of paint—everything dusty, dirty, cruddy. Are you out of your mind tellin' us you *love* that place?"

She explained, "It isn't the place. It's the lady that runs it. If you take her away, you have nothing but a barn and a bunch of nags."

At Parker's, anything you desired to do at any time could earn her sanction. If you wished to ride horseback at 4:30 A.M., you could.

"I'll meet you before dawn in the stable."

She'd ride with you. She'd moonlight ride. Ten o'clock at night. Full moon.

"Let's go riding!"

"Good!"

On the ride she'd recite poetry.

And sing.

Schedule played no part in Adele's world. If tired, she'd recline and take a nap. She could fall asleep in a twinkling and wake up refreshed. She simply did not care what time a thing was planned. When you did it, you did it. She could be

5

scheduled to lead a ride at eight A.M. but at eight A.M. someone would drive in with a chicken he didn't want.

Or someone would come around who was interesting for some insane reason. She would dab and poke at a thousand other projects before getting to the matter at hand. Meanwhile people paced up and down waiting to go. They couldn't understand *why,* when the appointment was for eight, the horses could not be ready and you could not go at *eight!*

It never happened.

Never.

A lot of it was simply a quirk in her nature. She didn't have a night and day in her life.

Some things, such as breeding horses, *were* reserved for the dark. At Parker's this usually was accomplished around three in the morning. Nobody could watch. And it occurred, she made sure, under the correct Astrological signs. Adele von Ohl Parker would scoop up any lingering children not yet in bed and rush them into the house. Then she would close all the doors and windows.

Private was private.

Numerous Parker alumni returned in later years with their own offspring. Edna Ettinger, like many others, was surprised when Mrs. P. would not hold the squawking infant. "Oh, I don't know about babies!" explained Adele von Ohl Parker.

"I really was surprised 'cause she loved kids so well," Edna Ettinger said a bit later. "But babies were unusual to her. I said, 'Well, they're just like puppies, Mrs. Parker. Just think of it as a little animal. . .' "

She believed stringently in taking things as they came, savoring each luscious hour, each unexpected happening. If she awoke in the morning to pouring rain and she couldn't do what she had planned to do—"OH, WHAT A LOVELY DAY! LOOK AT THAT BEAUTIFUL RAIN!"—*and really mean it* and just enjoy it thoroughly. "Well, this is the day to enjoy the rain! Another day we'll all enjoy *sunshine!* Another day we'll all enjoy snow!"

"She could be Lady Grande some days," her friend, Mary Rankin, said, "or she could be very childlike. A little girl. A

6

poor, penniless little child. A little waif. A little orphan. Or she could be the Indian chief. Or she could be the circus performer. She could lead the parade or be General Custer. She could be anybody. She could live in her imagination like nobody else.

"To *me*," Mary Rankin said, "Things simply have to *be*. . . I can't be happy in a world of dreams. It's got to come true and actually BE—or it doesn't mean anything. But for years Adele Parker could lie down on the top of her theater trunk and turn on the faucet in some mangy little fleabag dressing room backstage somewhere and let the faucet drip—and she would be happy dreaming she was lying alongside a churning, shimmering mountain stream where the silver spray gushed down the rocks.

"Is that sad? Or is it beautiful? She would do this. And wake up refreshed.

"As to conduct," Mary added, "she did not like kids getting the idea that because they were around a barn, they could use a lot of foul language and get that kind of rough, tough swagger and sass. It infuriated me when persons spoke of her as 'Ma Parker' or tried to make out that she was sort of a rough, tough western pre-hippy sort of thing.

"She had spent some time in the West, but in the West of those days, you had to be TERRIBLY ladylike. They were cut and dry and particular in their rules as to what a lady should be like. You might get by riding astride in Central Park, but in the West you had better have on a divided skirt and ride sidesaddle. And the girls in the West who rode sidesaddle rode sidesaddle on a regular western saddle—one knee hooked over the saddlehorn.

"It wasn't a *lady's* sidesaddle, such as you'd see in the park. And they'd wear long skirts, but they'd gather 'em up and wind 'em around somehow. There was none of this riding around in tight pants and slappin' the barnhands on the rear and all this rough talk that goes on in a lot of modern stables.

"It was simply out. She wouldn't have it."

The fat woman papering her ceiling said, "The only way I can describe her is to describe myself. I look like a slob. I run a messy house. I couldn't care less. There are more important things. The first time I met Adele Parker she was down in the barn with an old lumberman's parka on and a babushka around her head and her nose was running and she was pitching manure.

"I thought, 'Good God, is that a *woman?* What is it!' Principle she had a heap of, but she also said, "The hell with principle!" She did what she felt she *should* do and what she *wanted* to do, whether anyone felt it was just or not. Once committed, she plummeted ahead. Damn anybody who got in her way.

"What a cantankerous love of life! Her heart was a free agent. Her mind—fundamentalist:

" 'Black is black. White is white. The tree is green. God put the tree there for a purpose. I'm going to enjoy this tree. If I have to, I'll make use of it. That's why it was put there.' Talk got pretty deep sometimes. 'There is something more over the hill. I've got to see what it is. There's something more in people. I've got to find out what is in people. What makes them love, cheat, be afraid, understand. . .'

"She wasn't afraid of anything."

Parker referred to herself as a gypsy type. The green wagon near the ring was called a "caravan." Everybody knew it by that name. It never moved. Once it was a parttime office but most of the time, just sleeping quarters. In it lay her prized tanned horsehide throw rug, once part of a horse named Flying Fish, who wouldn't mind.

She was to Robert Gump of Berea, Ohio, "all the things no one else was or could be—or would even allow, God knows! My grandmother," said Gump, "is a doctor, my great grandmother a nurse, her brother a dentist. When I was a child I couldn't have a kitten unless it was scrubbed three-quarters to death. So I'd go out to Parker's for overnights. Parker would pull something out of her saddlebag—black, gritty, full of glass, and throw it in the fire—turning it now and again with a manure fork. It was delicious."

She had, it was said, "a Greenwich Village intelligence." She knew how to work people, how to motivate them. She was all sparks *that* way. She was hardly "smart" as one un-

8

derstands the word. Someone once asked her to spell raccoon. She said, "R-a-t-e... ratoon," which suggests she was also partly deaf.

Parker was as sharp as she was dull. And Parker's Ranch was a contradiction to everything.

"Mrs. Parker was wonderful," said some people, "but she was a dog."

"Kindness," her psychologist friend insisted, "isn't a word I would ever apply to her. Basically, I suppose it was kindness. I would rather have called it concern. She had an incredible respect for life, and whether it was kind or not I think never really bothered her one way or another. Life in itself was important. And life was to be preserved. And life was to live. She found people lacking much of the time but she had great respect for the potential. Always the *potential!*"

Adele did not—*would* not—tolerate sympathy in any fashion. If she broke an arm, it simply made her mad. It robbed her of a day. If she broke a rib, it was ridiculous! Nobody should have to put up with such a silly thing! She never wished to miss an hour. She was like a bolt of lightning—perpetually crashing and sparking and thundering.

The thing I never understood was her consistent cordiality to me—to *me,* lower in the ranch hierarchy than the most casual Sunday rider. Again and again she caught me flat, so surprised and stunned was I. She'd say, "C'mon! C'mon along! Get a horse and c'mon! Hop on the wagon and c'mon! Sit up here and talk to me!"

And could she talk! Could she quote poetry—oh, my, yes—by the ream! She drove and I sat at her back. Not beside her. People didn't sit beside her as she drove. She wanted no one next to her. The place of honor was at her back. Then while she, with her hawk eyes, scanned the road for danger and controlled her horses, she would talk over her shoulder to me.

She was, I believe, looking always for Indians somewhere up ahead.

At Halloween we fixed up the Geezle barn as a spook house—the best one anyone ever had in the world. Somebody

9

played the piano and we had pieces of soaked liver hanging on strings which struck you in the face as you walked through. Eugenia, Mrs. Parker's beautiful trainer, wore her flaxen hair unbraided and long. She put flour or something on it. Here's this gorgeous girl—the best lookin' witch I ever saw, with tall, pointed hat and exciting bleached tresses. Mrs. Parker had a wonderful time. She went through our spookhouse twenty-nine times and howled and scared us to death.

When they buried Chester and Danny Boy and another horse back in the archery pit, everybody knew their ghosts were down there, all right. Adele had whispered it to a confidant. Kids would go down on Halloween to see the ghosts walk the archery pit. But we wouldn't go down at night. Even Bob Gump wouldn't go down at night.

Pretty Jackie Loehr Kaesgen of Brookpark smiled as she reflected. "I spent my Christmas vacations out there," she said. "I slept at home, I think, but other than that I stayed in the manger with Phantom, my horse, and read books, and he would get food by rooting for it down under the hay. He was so like a big puppy, that slop of a horse—not beautiful. . . You'd sit in front of him and he'd put his head in your lap.

"You'd scratch his ears and tell him how poor he was. He'd quiver and make horrible noises, my lovely big slob. He'd untie his rope and get into the corncrib and you'd have to haul him out of it. He supposedly came from Mrs. Parker's Mac Donald line stallions that roguishly bred with a cast-off mare from the circus.

"Phantom was the result. A big hulky nut, a little bit wise, a little bit funny."

Jackie grinned.

"He would dump me off in a particular corner—on purpose. I'd let him go out without a halter into the ring and just let him go and he'd flip me off in the one corner where he always pretended to be afraid. So it was routine. He'd run around and scream like a stallion, which he wasn't. Then I'd get back on. Just a clown. That's all. He kind of fit with the ranch."

10

Adele insisted upon one thing all of the time: honesty. A fella came there once and commenced to tell us all about horses in the West. He knew it all. Parker picked him a horse that was one long snort of fire and said, "There he is. Take him." She purposely left the cinch loose. Of course the saddle slid when he went to board up. Parker was on him in a stroke—"I THOUGHT YOU KNEW ABOUT RIDING! *FIRST* THING A RIDER DOES IS TO SEE IF HIS CINCH IS TIGHT!"

In two minutes she pressed him to admit he didn't know anything at all, not even his poor name. Parker could tell in a half dozen sentences with a person whether they *liked* horses and *knew* horses. Many she turned down (in the hardest of hard times) who came there to ride. She chatted with them a moment. . .

No, she was sorry. She had no horses available.

In reality, the ranch belonged to us all. It was a feeling we all had. It was a hiding place, a secret palace with a dirty face. Sometimes it would be bitter cold and customers would be pulling in in cars. Parker would "wink" and we'd send them away. And if riders got smart with us—especially teen-agers—she'd say, "Business like that we don't need! Bring 'em back! Just turn around and bring 'em back!" And we did—plenty of times! She wasn't interested in the money at all.

There was room enough for a swimming pool in the lot where Parker inevitably built her ring. The clay and materials to make a high bank around it were all heaped up ready for action, but we could see it could really never come about, no matter what. What happened was a certain party (who incidentally disappeared with amnesia and was finally discovered in Columbus, Ohio) blew the whistle on her alleged "unsanitary conditions" because we had been getting by with an outside doolie (it was just as clean as her kitchen counter, if you care to know the truth).

But oh, no. She was running a public place. She had to have proper facilities. Of course, our swimming pool capital went into the construction of that ridiculous john.

On various and seemingly cyclic occasions, her acreage

11

was overrun by litters of cats. For the lot of them, Adele provided a portion of the barn, put a little red light out front and called it her pretty cat house. Add to that fifteen Pomeranian dogs, the products of incest. One appeared constantly to be walking down hill. All the dogs stemmed from one somewhat worldly bitch which Adele (fairly characteristically) had named "Cherry."

Every time you turned around, Cherry had another pup. Who was the father? Oh, Bobo or David. David was the most revolting dog. Once he jumped off the couch, broke every bone in his body, and gave up the ghost. Mrs. Parker breathed life back into him. "How," asked a stranger on what proved to be short loan, "could one ever get close enough to put one's mouth into that revolting, smelly little thing?"

(To the best of anyone's memory, the stranger was never again seen in the vicinity of Parker's Ranch.)

Someone counted seventeen Pomeranians at one point. Big ones. Cockeyed ones. Bow-legged ones.

They all sang.

When we had a party or something, the kids would throw watermelon rhines to the pig. Some kids would aim at and hit the pig and hurt it. God, how she lectured on why you shouldn't hurt the pig. *The pig isn't there to hurt!* It is something to *enjoy!* It is a *living thing!* She'd break your goddam head if she caught you doing it again. For she loved the pig. She loved everything.

The ranch was called upon to supply animals for all occasions, which was how Sybil, the beautiful guernsey, came to be trucked down to the Carter Hotel in downtown Cleveland. The Dairyman's Association wanted the live, contented muncher at its luncheon. There was to be television coverage. Someone mentioned Parker's.

"Beautiful Sybil!" sighed on of the ranchers. "She had a face like Elsie, the Borden trademark, "but prettier." Anyway, they wanted a cow. There was a catch. The cow had to be housebroken. Parker could handle problems like that. She knew how to feed properly and precisely when to water. She cleaned out old Syb before we took off. Even so, she took no

12

chances. The night before, Adele made her a diaper. Should there *be* an accident, it would be caught. Well, we all climbed in and Mrs. P. drove Sybil downtown to the hotel.

That's where she dressed the cow in the diaper. Sybil was indeed groomed and polished and beautiful. Adele von Ohl Parker led her in through the lobby and bystanders fell all over themselves.

Then Parker and the cow were on television. Sybil was doing so fine. It got time to go. We led her out to the elevator.

Now an animal is an animal. You can do so much toward cleaning them out but there is a limit to their endurance. We were pressing our luck hard, so for once, Mrs. Parker was exhuberant when it came time to go. Then the newsmen wanted some pictures. The women brought Sybil back up to the dining room. Mrs. Parker, by now, was doing mental arithmetic, but Sybil held her own.

Finished with the cameras, we all led Sybil into the elevator, down to the lobby, out to the sidewalk. Everyone breathed happy. Parker took the unsoiled diaper off, got Sybil loaded, put up the tailgate.

Somebody came out.

"Hey, we need her back in there!" he shouted.

We took Sybil out of the trailer, put the diaper back on, tied it in a bow, took her back into the hotel, up the elevator, and out among hundreds of conventioners. For a full hour more Sybil showed a bravery and inner discipline that made even Adele von Ohl Parker wince.

But while Sybil was serene, her three-year-old castrated son Sebelius, a Jersey bull, got pretty nasty early in life, what with breeding back its mother all the time. Parker could never figure when the signs were right.

One very hot day, Sebelius was chasing Sybil, his own mother, in the front pasture, and if you've ever seen a cow running, it's nothing but swinging bags and clattering hooves and go-go-go, and old Sybil simply fell down from exhaustion. About that time the police drove by and told Eugenia they were going to report her to the humane society for running those animals three-quarters to death. All the girl had been trying to do when the police butted in was to save the goddam cow! So she simply sat down and sobbed hysterically.

Sybil was the kind of cow that had no milk. I can remember Helen Duncan down there trying to milk Sebelius. She'd grab a tit and say, "*Look* at that healthy thing! It's so wonderful, but nothing's coming out! No one recalls what happened to Sybil but Mary kept raising Sebelius who finally went the way of all steers.

It was a lovely roast and there was jello for dessert.

Old riders still recall how smooth Sybil was. Better than Shanks Mare, anyway. . . "Shanks Mare"—a favorite expression. Parker really was referring to your own two feet, see? She'd say, "Tomorrow I'm going to put you on a real *good* horse—you're going to ride Shanks Mare!" She had talked so much about Starlight and Chester—we thought, "Shanks Mare?" Wow, you know? She'd tell beginners, "Wait til we get you on Shanks Mare!"

Adele had at the ranch a bunch of turkeys and a flock of pea hens—grey hens with small heads. The hens had it down to a science. They'd go clucking along back of some unsuspecting soul. The person would look over his shoulder and of course it would worry him that this pair of birds was four steps behind him. He'd therefore walk faster and the birds would walk faster. He'd start to run—the hens would run. And they would peck in considerable earnest at his heels.

One of these chickens wandered into Hezzikiah the mule's pen and the first thing we noticed was that Hezzie was running in circles and wouldn't stop. He had this chicken cornered in his pen and every time he'd go by, the mule'd stick his foot out and after two dozen rounds of that, he'd killed the chicken—*mutilated* it, anyway. It happened in the days when Old Jack (the man on the Cream of Wheat box) was cooking at Parker's.

Jack finished him off. It all happened in the morning and we had it for lunch. He made soup. Cream of chicken soup.

One of the true marvels of Parker's was the training of the ranch cats. Mama cat would take the kittens from the very outset and train them to behave around horses. It was some-

14

thing to watch. But then people would come out there with their domesticated kittens and dump them. Invariably they were smashed. I mean literally crushed in the barns because they did not know how to get around.

One day Chico stepped on one. I remember running up to the house, crying, "Take it to a vet! Take it to a vet!" She said, calmly, "There's nothing we can do. Half its brains are smashed." She laid it gently on the dusty ground and destroyed it with three bullets.

Horses' heads at her dining room window were common fare for the plumber's wife, Jean McKenna, next door, as was the pig that got loose on Mastick Road.

"The county engineers were repaving and patching the road while the pig ran back and forth in the middle of the street," Jean still recalls.

"It happened a week before Mrs. Parker died. I ran over there screaming that the pig was out front. Oh, I'll never forget it. She was lying on the couch and kind of in a daze. I ran into the house crying, 'Mrs. Parker! Mrs. Parker! Clemmie's in the street and these cars are blowing horns!' and—oh, I'll never forget it—this pig just stood there with all that commotion and all, and of course, people are scared because a pig will attack you.

"The county people stayed in their trucks. Here were dozens of cars with their horns blowing, their drivers yelling. Mrs. Parker said, so weakly, 'What?' And I said again, 'Clemmie's out on the road!'

"Usually, she'd have boomed out there like nothin', but she just didn't get up at first. She was in this daze—like. Finally I just kept telling her over and over, 'What shall I do?' while trying to get her up. She did come out. She fetched something—a stick, perhaps—and went out with the hired hands, two old, old fellas. . ."

The pig was the first item shipped out the driveway after Mrs. Parker's death. There was no ceremony.

At Parker's Ranch, Mary and Mrs. Parker and certain others were pretty hep people. I mean they didn't think "Dostoevsky" was a disease. They were familiar with him. Mrs. P. loved poetry but rarely was observed with a book. In

15

fact they believed in little, intellectually. Mrs. Parker's remark to the priests—"The *world* is my cathedral... nature and this valley!" She was not sure that there was God, yet she eternally bent to a spiritual direction. She knew life was more than just animals humping.

Toward the end she could no longer express things, could not be sufficiently forceful or as symbolic as she was earlier. So her youth faded, not her philosophy, not her intent. The animals out there became old and chronic—like Mrs. Parker—and seemingly on the same time scale.

She still languished in her dream state and everybody went along and played up the good, while privately acknowledging that the bad was sitting down there, too. And though she had ideas of grandeur, she had neither the ability nor inclination to carry them out. Oh, she'd tour the cities that Cody toured... she was a great dreamer. She could *dream* of doing that.

If you could *believe,* it was beautiful. Choose to look at it practically, it wasn't. That's what it always came down to. She asked some of us in the quadrille to go with her and tour the West and put on something or other for an act. Then someone I never saw before walked up to her one April afternoon and cruelly and maliciously announced that her day was gone.

I consider it no overstatement to conclude that on that same afternoon, Adele von Ohl Parker began the long and messy process of death.

"We'd talk," the truck driver said, "of how kids were brought up years ago. Things they had to do. We'd talk of some animal outside or something like that. I asked her a couple of times if she ever wanted me to take her anyplace. She had trouble with her car and rather than get a halfway decent one, she always had somebody putter with it.

"Once, coming down Kennedy Ridge, I came upon Mrs. Parker in her car going first off the road, then back on, then off, then on... At first I didn't recognize her. I saw the station wagon but I thought, no—then I recognized her, for I knew just how she sat in a seat.

"But her face—she looked dead.

16

"I went home very ill."

"I'd like to write about her spirit," Parker's old friend, Jean Tomer said. "Just some short thing."

"How are you going to do that, Jean?" said another.

"Oh, I've felt it all these years."

"How are you going to put it into words?"

"I can't. I'll have to find the distance. I started to write something about Mrs. Parker once. You reach a point where you're dealing with the ethereal... where you're just——floating around..."

"We all put people on pedestals," her friend said. "As we grow older, they may shrink. And we object to this. We don't ever want them to shrink. We want them right out there, forever."

Thundering into the ring at every Parker's Ranch extravaganza, Adele would hike her stallion to its hind legs and wave to the ever-present throng. For years Parker's was a continuous *Land of Make-Believe,* and little of the real world could touch it. Newspaper people, caught up in the spirit, played "Indians" along with her. "*The Plain Dealer's* Jan Mellow once had to hit the dirt along with the rest of us," one of the Parker kids explained "The Indians were coming and if you didn't go down, Parker knocked you down. When those Indians rode for your head, you dropped to all fours."

CHAPTER 2

LAST TRAIN FROM PLAINFIELD

Hard facts about Adele are not plentiful. Dates are sketchy. The specifics of events have been dimmed by time and the thinning out of reputable witnesses. A few have come forth and offered testimony.

According to the local write-up by Ingrid Gilbert (who was as hypnotized by the Grande Dame as any of us) of the *West Side News*, a Cleveland suburban newspaper, the von Ohl family began importing fine horses into the U.S. in 1682. The strains they developed (she swears) rendered valuable scout service to George Washington during the Revolution. Mrs. Parker's home state, New Jersey, (she swears further) honored these horses in the state seal which shows the head ·of a black stallion.

A Xerox copy of a page from Van Wyck Brooks' *Scenes and Portraits: Memories of Childhood and Youth* (Dutton, 1954), prompted me to buy an airplane ticket to Plainfield, New Jersey, to visit Adele's grown-up childhood playmate, Dorothy Fyfe, who resided in neighboring Edison and who jumped horses while in her seventies. I went to ask her about ghosts and turtles.

Author Brooks had written, "How many odd characters, how many queer folk there seemed to be (after the Civil War in every country neighborhood), as many as one found in Russian novels of Tolstoy, which we had in the house—types that vanished in later days into sanitariums or were smoothed out by psychoanalysts.

"For instance" Brooks wrote, "there were the von Ohls, reputedly well-born Germans who had fallen upon evil days and drove into town, to market, in a ramshackle gypsy trap and who lived in a rotting old house on the edge of a swamp in the woods that always evoked the story of *No Haid Pawn.* For there was a pond near by this breeding-place for ghosts and a gigantic bloodhound that rushed out once at Max Perkins and me when we were searching in the swamp for turtles.

"We stood back to back, half expecting a horrible death, only to discover that the old hound was toothless. . ."

In Plainfield, New Jersey, I observed with Dorothy Fyfe that same dark pond.

"How far back in time does the von Ohl homestead date, Mrs. Fyfe?"

"There isn't anyone alive who would remember that because the family was so looked down upon. Brooks implies that—and he is right."

"You mean there was a disregard for theater people?"

"Indeed, so! The von Ohls were theater people and they were also horse people. And of course Plainfield, New Jersey, was no less the home of the hundred dollar millionaires, thus the von Ohls were ignored completely. My mother and the von Ohl family used to ride together in the parades. I remember so well that my father had a full beard and he would put on an Uncle Sam's hat and hitch up one of the old horses. The South Lincoln Hose Department would be with us—something that Adele thought up for fun. Sometimes we rode in the von Ohl's basket cart pulled by two small ponies. Adele would put bunting around the spokes and mother would drive. . ."

"Could this be the cart Brooks called a 'gypsy trap?'"

"Perhaps, but if so, it was an ignorant mistake. Basket carts, far from ragbag, were tremendously expensive then. They're rare today."

We walked in the wet grass through Cedar Park, keeping an eye cocked for snapping turtles in that pond of ponds, a rock's throw from where the old house stood in 1900.

"What do you remember of the homestead?"

"It was yellow and had a porch all the way around. It was in no way ornate. Not a bit. A two-story place. Of course, I wasn't interested in the house then. It was always the horses. There were always a few there. On Halloween night, Adele and her sister Winnona dressed up in sheets and rode horseback through the colored section of Plainfield. I remember her telling me, much out of breath, that she frightened them all and they fell in a ditch."

Exclaimed Dorothy, "She also spoke of an old great

grandfather—grandfather Laing—who had been a scout for General Washington. She told of tying her horse at Willow Lake; of returning to find the animal out of its head with fear—fighting, plunging, lunging! She later discovered that the spot was where Captain Laing regularly dismounted. Servants claimed to have seen the ghost. Always others. Never she. So many times I helped her look but we did not find the hoof marks though we looked often enough, if not well enough, for a man on a horse, transparent or otherwise."

I told Dorothy Fyfe of my letter of inquiry to W. Gale Hoffman of The Historical Society of Plainfield and North Plainfield, asking for some professional snooping into the von Ohl ancestry. Little of significance turned up, though the Society president questioned his way through nursing homes and other places searching for owners of long memories. And he uncovered a few.

One woman claimed "long and scandalous memories of the von Ohls." She recalled they were aristocrats who lost everything and became quite suddenly poor, but regained their regal bearing. Another said "the lot of them were on their uppers. Perfectly snooty!"

"Well," Mrs. Fyfe suggested, "they (the town) was snooty in return. Yes, they were *all* snoots!"

"And these same persons say the von Ohl's sudden status of poverty was most apparent; that they came to town in dusty, tattered clothes. . . in dirty, unkept, careless attire—in a pony cart or governor's cart. . ."

"No! No! I told you. . . They didn't have a governor's cart!"

". . . And horsedrawn—with dogs running to the rear and alongside. . ."

"No! No! No! I am positive the people were senile; their imaginations had gotten the best of them. They had no right to say such things because the von Ohls were a *respectable* family who simply kept to themselves. It wasn't a matter of *before* the Depression or *after* the Depression, the von Ohls were *always* depressed. As long as I can remember, there was never a time they were affluent in any way. Why do you suppose Adele went out and worked?"

"Because," said I, "dozens of reviews make clear she was a rebel from eastern society."

"What the heck!" wailed Dorothy Fyfe, "she WAS no society!"

"She was," I quoted, " 'the early day anti-establishment.' But. . . maybe it began with something she said to someone. . ."

"That's it—then like a snowball. . ."

". . . into the newspaper morgue!"

"Yes, and of course for publicity sake, it came in very handy. I can see that. A rebel? Come to think of it, I suppose she *was,* because she had to go out and work and if you've got to go out and dig *that* young, you've got to say to hell with everybody and not care a rap what *anyone* says!"

Whatever the world and Plainfield, New Jersey, thought of the family von Ohl, there can be little question of the critical acclaim earned by Adele in her debut performance as an actress at the Reform Hall Theater, right in her own backyard.

In a *Plainfield Courier-News* article entitled, "MADE HER BOW TO THE PUBLIC," carried on February 22, 1902, the town's theatrical critic wrote, "Adele von Ohl's first appearance as a professional actress may be considered a triumph, for almost every one of her long speeches was followed by a burst of hand-clapping, and the close of every act was met by the audience with an instant demand for her appearance before the curtain. . . She carried herself with the poise of a professional. . . it was apparent that only practice is necessary to fit her for a place with the best companies. Several times during the course of the performance the feminine portion of the audience witnessed the action of the play over the tops of soppy handkerchiefs and listened to the speeches between sniffles."

But backstage and on the street in public was another matter. Applause and recognition were reserved for the darkened playhouse, the narrow theatrical runway before the footlights.

"Actresses," Dorothy Fyfe said, "were badgered, snubbed and avoided due to unreasoned prejudice. Later on, I was an actress as well and was quite aware of it. You entered the back door of a restaurant. You went into the back door of a hotel. You often were turned down by hotels altogether."

"Did it matter how well known you were?"

"Not at all."

"And you're speaking not only of vaudeville, but the legitimate theater?"

"Oh, yes. I used to work with a theater company and usually we were accepted in only the worst hotels. I shall never forget one of them in which I was compelled to stand on top of a dresser and leap upon the bed, so thick were the carpet fleas. We were charged the regular price, however. I know very well how Adele must have been treated. She was on stage before I was in show business, thus it must have been *worse* for her. And of course a horse is an animal and——phew! You know, it sticks to you. . .

"But Adele was *always* up to something," Dorothy Fyfe laughed. "She tried so hard to do things to bring in money for her family. Like plowing a victory garden—with albino Arabian horses, for God's sake!"

"She kept up her interest in legitimate theater?"

"She was interested in everything! But I'm sure she realized after a little while that she was to be the family mainstay. When she did marry, the mother was unhappy. We often questioned whether it was because of Jim Parker *personally,* or simply that the financial fountain was about to be plugged.

"Adele was a very *sweet* person. I wondered then how she managed to keep so clean. Her hair was shiny and tied up in a bun. She had a square jaw. Very sharp brown eyes. Lovely dark eyebrows. When she went on the road, I was quite young and thoroughly horsey. Later, what appeared as Adele's own troupe came home. They were getting set for an appearance in Plainfield and one in Westfield. Of course I hung around. Adele baited my mother to let me go with her, but being a hard-shelled Baptist she wouldn't listen to it. Of course I saw the show anyway. I was a soft-shelled Baptist. I remember sitting around a simulated campfire singing 'Pony Boy' and 'Redwing,' and Adele blowing in on a horse.

"Adele was *forever* thinking up things to do. We had a

great day of fun charging about the place in a stagecoach borrowed from her company. There simply had to be action when she was home. When Adele's mother died, my apprentice blacksmith was asked to do something unheard of in these parts. He was called to the von Ohl home and told to nail an iron horseshoe to the coffin lid."

"The von Ohls really half worked for and were half guests of the New Jersey industrialist, Pierre Lorrelard, in Georgetown," added Adele's cousin, Dolly Bateman, "though Adele liked to plant the impression that they were on equal footing. I know her mother believed in spirits and second sight and things of that character. I recall an instance in particular in which she sensed an impression of a complete translation of an Egyptian inscription. The next day a noted Egyptologist published it in the newspaper."

Skittering references to southern plantations wove through hundreds of Mrs. Parker's conversations down the years, but almost like ghosts, like filmy memories. At times it was as though her mother—as though someone—had told her, "You really came from better than this." You kept having the feeling about Adele and Winnona von Ohl that they had seen all those beautiful people second hand and were clinging to the memory, but that it wasn't real to them, it hadn't substance. In other ways, strangely, they appeared to put themselves above it all, saying, "I can't have it so I don't want it."

In earlier days the horse was king of the avenue. It was a great time for shows and Adele von Ohl turned her hand to anything that promised a little excitement and a good ride. In 1905 she "arrived" at the new Hippodrome Theater in New York. After that she divided her time among high society; jumping horses at Atlantic City's Million Dollar Pier; featuring with the great Buffalo Bill; and being billed as the highest paid actress in New York.

Her way of living was all her own, incomprehensible and incredible for that time. Whether at a debutante's tea or in a sawdust ring, she had a good showman's knack for doing the unexpected. The New York Hippodrome had a horse plunging act in which riders took their horses off a runway into a twenty foot tank of water. The act featured "15 men and one slim girl who couldn't swim." The latter, of course, was Adele von Ohl. On three occasions during the running of that act, she deliberately turned a somersault in mid-air to avoid striking seven or eight struggling horses and riders already in the tank.

Forty-two years afterward, showman Billy Rose's story of 50 elephants stampeding the streets of New York in 1907 brought a frothy 49-elephant correction from the saucy showwoman, who called *Cleveland Press* columnist Joe Collier.

"One elephant only escaped from the old Hippodrome Theater on that stirring day," assured Collier the following day, "and forgetful of all but his terror ran down 5th Avenue in full flight from the primitive action on the theater stage."

"Mrs. Parker knows because she was there. Perched 40 feet high on the ledge of the Proscenium Arch, a seat adapted only to one of her brimming spirit, she looked down on the vast stage at the experimental introduction of two strange herds of trained elephants.

"Mrs. Parker was widely celebrated there as Adele von Ohl, a rebellious eastern society girl, expert with horses and the star of the spectacular stage... But the restless management, always in search of marginal novelties, wanted 50 elephants as well. And the owners of two herds, persuaded by sensational wads of money to act against their own gloomy predictions. brought the beasts together to see what would happen. From her Olympian perch, Adele saw the two herds enter from opposite sides. They stopped short when they noticed each other. The leaders trumpeted. And the whole theater jumped with their searching challenges.

"Then they charged and the actress looked down on jungle warfare. Out of the tumult Mrs. Parker could occasionally isolate individual feats of bravado. She saw one elephant scoop up another with tusk and trunk and toss it over his head to land stunned on the stage. She caught another cut out of the mass by a combat team of three, each with a trunk around one of its legs and made unfit for action as they lumbered him around and around in tight circles.

25

"For almost an hour the stampede continued. The trainers gave unheeded commands from the fringe of battle. They were effectual only in guiding retreating beasts to their off-stage quarters and securing them there. The one elephant that ran clear of all restraints charged down 5th Avenue, turned into a residential section and tried to hide in a frame tenement house, getting himself stuck, stormily, in the doorway. . ."

In 1909, Adele married Jim Parker, an extraordinary horseman in the Buffalo Bill troupe. They celebrated their union by appearing the next session in a show bearing the heart-quickening name, "Cheyenne Days."

They played all over the U.S. for five years, a mixture of one-night stands, weekly engagements, and appearances at fairs which once were the drawing cards of every county seat. Adele always recalled the period with much sentiment and tears. Their appearance on the narrow stages in use at that time gave a real thrill to pedestrian audiences.

It was even more thrilling to the musicians playing in the pit before the stage. The music for "Cheyenne Days" used to come back to the Parkers at the end of the season annotated by the fiddle players.

At certain bars of music would appear written in pencil, "Get out of the pit here if you value your life!"

It was no mere joke.

The orchestra well remembered Adele's act where she portrayed an artist and a huge horse would come charging through her easel as she painted. Somehow he slipped—and she slipped. She fell into the orchestra pit with the heavy animal on top of her . . . both falling on top of the cello player. She indeed was very much a medical phenomenon in that at one time or other, she had practically every bone in her body broken by a horse. The cello player never played again, either.

That is why the musicians scrambled from the pit and played in the aisles as Adele Parker's horse reared and screamed above them on the stage. It was known about the circuit that horses with reputations as killers and outlaws were apple pie for this strange woman, but few cared to share her dessert.

In the spring of 1914, the entire troupe of Cheyenne Days went to Europe to give the effete capitals a glimpse of the old frontier. They were booked for a tour of the entire continent by Morris & Stahl, a European agency similar in prestige to the old Keith-Albee circuit. In the coliseum in London, they played before an audience which had among its distinguished members King George and Queen Mary. But the European insanity which first infected the continent forced them to scuttle home and to consider themselves fortunate to get a ship.

During the years Mrs. Parker played across the country, she incurred a debt of gratitude from that leading exponent of the horse opera, Tom Mix. It came about when Adele reluctantly refused his request for a berth with the show. Fine rider that he was, the troupe was filled. Adele von Ohl Parker sobbed into her handkerchief a while (she could, it was said, produce a tear and squirt it clear across a river). Then she took out pen and paper and personally wrote Mix a letter of introduction to her producer friends in California, whereupon Tom Mix, another easterner from New Jersey, went to Hollywood where he earned celluloid immortality as the quintessence of the Old West.

Another wayfarer whose path crossed that of Mrs. Parker was Roscoe Fatty Arbuckle who played with the show for a short time before becoming successively famous and infamous. His instinct for comedy led him to inject touches in Cheyenne Days that were never taken out.

A candid caricature of horse theater of her day can be appreciated by this report, headed, HEAVY STAGING AT PANTAGES, which appeared in the *Spokesman Review* in Spokane:

"Alf MacAlpine and his deckhands backstage at Pantages Theater this week are the busiest performers on the bill and they work without applause and almost entirely behind the scenes. The current offering, according to Manager E. Clarke Walker, is the heaviest, scenically, the theater has ever housed. Three of the five acts use the full stage with heavy scenic equipment. The stage crew worked most of the night

27

'hanging' the show and set it five times yesterday.

"Adele von Ohl, a stately horsewoman, popular with Pantages patrons, heads "The Texas Round-up," considerably the biggest horse act seen on a local vaudeville stage. There are cowboys, cowgirls, a colored cook, a real Indian, buckaroos, a donkey, a bucking bronco and a dozen horses in the offering. It is surprising the realistic results the company scores on the limited stage area.

"Expert marksmanship, smart dressage, singing and dialogue are featured by Max Le Hoen and Leone Dupreece. Miss Dupreece does sensational target work with a small rifle from the balcony, extinguishing candles on the stage. Her partner rings bells with his bullets, playing an accompaniment to her singing.

"An actual working model of a Marconi wireless telegraph is a novelty in the comedy skit, "A Corner In Wireless," featuring Dan Bruce as the operator and Margo Duffet as the sweetheart, with C.O. Glover as the stern parent. The wireless flashes and sputters vividly on the roof of a skyscraper overlooking New York harbor and is the pivot of a brisk comedy drama.

"Harry Adler and Anna Arline burlesque the serious hypnotists, Adler coming from the audience and working as the subject. While "under the influence," he impersonates animals and birds and imitates their vocal efforts in striking fashion.

"Frank Weber, Fred Beck and Jack Frazer are musical entertainers of the familiar collegian type, marring some very pleasing vocal work with a surplus of exaggerated nut comedy. Their offering pleased the Sunday crowds just the same and they were called back several times. . ."

Later, Adele Parker moved on to Hollywood where she made stunt horseback riding motion pictures, tripling as actress, stunt man, and coach. Her contract called for teaching silent screen cowboys how to shoot, ride and fall from a horse in a manner that appeared the height of daredeviltry on film.

Meanwhile, having had his fill of the jam-packed tents, theaters, and motion picture lots, Jim Parker lit out for his sheriff father's ranch in Montana to get his wind and to think things out. One day, soon afterward, he sent Adele a telegram:

"BOUGHT 300 WILD HORSES. BETTER COME HOME AND HELP BRING THEM IN."

Up to this point, Adele had performed daredevil rides in practically every state in the union and in all parts of Europe. She had ridden her famous performing horses before every President of the United States from Cleveland to Coolidge. She knew the spine-tapping thrill of riding in steeplechases, horse shows, vaudeville, circuses and the movies, but rounding up wild horses in the badlands and training them to ride was another matter. That was the thrill of a lifetime.

With Jim's telegram clutched in her hand, she simply walked off the movie lot and caught the first train heading north. Several years later, a story titled, "My First Wild Horse Hunt," by Adele von Ohl Parker, was run in serial form in *Rider and Driver Magazine,* a New York publication. The year was 1929, and the literary exercise was one of few available examples of Adele's vigor and freshness of expression in essay form. It furnishes a stimulating account of wildness, solitude and nature that is both breathtaking and childlike in its quality. It is particularly interesting to note that the author never graduated from grammar school:

MY FIRST WILD HORSE HUNT

by Adele von Ohl Parker

"It was in Montana at Dad Parker's ranch on Tongue River one mile from the Decker post office. The one building at Decker was the general store, dance hall and church, literary and political headquarters. I believe Decker is on the map if you can find the right map. It is twenty-three miles northeast from Sheridan, Wyoming, on a windy day——the longest twenty-three miles ever covered.

"Miles don't count in Montana. It is just 'how long 'til we get there?' The ice was flowing down river in great crashing cakes and the bluebirds were just arriving. The wildflowers were in their height of fashion and the frogs had ceased their croaking.

"Now this was a real ranch—a cowman's home. And you can never tell how rich a cowman is by the size of his house or by what he wears. The ranch buildings included a nice two-room frame building, well painted, joined to a log cabin of one room. Nearby was a toolroom, newly built, everything neat as a pin. Also there was a coal room. They mine their own soft coal on the place. The stable, or barn, speaking properly in Montana, was well-built and would stable ten head of stock. In the rear were haystacks and a nice house. To one side was a large round corral built of heavy smooth timbers with great posts closely set together and eight 12-inch planks to a panel set so you could just get your hand between.

"This was necessary for breaking horses, also for milking wild cows. The house was about a hundred feet from the river, surrounded by great tall cottonwoods. Across the river were rugged hills and cut banks dotted with jack pines and the perfume of the willow blossoms, sweet grasses and crisp, high air.

"It was far from lonesome.

"I had planned to stay two weeks. After a few days watching Jim and Dad break wild horses they had captured before my arrival, I knew I could stay forever. I realized Jim had used the same method to capture me.

"One afternoon Jim said, 'We are going after more tomorrow.'

"Wild horses held that certain something for me that is totally unexplainable. As a child I pretended to be a wild horse, the unconquerable, while other children would be the willing work horse. I felt the wild horse spirit and now was my chance to make all my dreams come true. On a morn remindful of Charles M. Russell's paintings of Montana, we started—Dad, Jim, and myself.

"Dad was mounted on an old chunky gray horse, Dick, leading another called Bob—two perfect stock horses. Jim's mount was a green horse, Lonnie, and he led another named Slim—a great prospect for a high jumper. He had jumped out of our corral three times. He was the only horse I ever begged Jim not to try to break 'cause he never seemed to look at you—just *through you*. But after he was broke, he was a great one.

"I was mounted on a well-built, fleet mare—Dimples, and was leading another, very much the same type, only faster. Both had been captured the same time as Lonnie. Neither had been ridden more than five or six times. I had packed a big lunch, camera, canteen, an extra sweater in case we had to sleep out all night. Also a slicker and a rope.

"When Jim saw this pack on the green, half-broken steed, he started to clean house. Dad packed three sandwiches in the saddle pockets and the only thing left me was the rope.

"This is no picnic. This is work. No excess," Jim said.

"Well, I smuggled three oranges in case of thirst. Riding while the sun was between the earth and center sky, Dad got off every now and then to search the surrounding country through his field glasses. We were on an upward grade way up in the Deercreek Mountains, a small range but rough country. Never saying a word to one another we opened out coats as the sun got higher. Never speaking is a good idea. You don't get thirsty so soon. But it was hard for me when I wanted to know so much.

"I tried to memorize the lay of the land so as to know the way home on a horse that knew only the open ranges. About high noon, Dad stopped again. We were on a high ridge that seemed to divide two worlds—one full of vegetation and the other of burnt-out, lifeless, forsaken badland country. I was certain I would be the one to locate these wild horses and I knew just how I would see them—all running and playing, tossing their manes, snorting, jumping and kicking. I looked 'til a film formed over my eyes from not winking, fearing one wink would be the cause of not finding them first.

"Then Dad calmly said, 'There they are,' putting his field glasses back in his saddle pockets.

"Where?" I cried.

"There!" cried he, slowly pointing westward.

"I followed his pointing finger, expecting to find some right away. But no, not one could be seen.

"Jim said, 'Don't you see them over there? Way over there on that knoll?'

31

"It was hard to believe a bunch of wild horses would have been so well groomed by nature to have shone like that. They stood two miles away, basking in the sun, swishing flies from one another's face.

" 'We'll change horses,' Jim said.

"I thought they would be gone in the meantime—flying, running. But we changed and rode on as quietly as if we had plenty of time for church. My heart was pumping faster. I did not feel stiff in the knees. I was not thirsty and it was not hot. Everything was perfect except that Jim and Dad rode so slowly. I could hardly believe it when Dad called another time out. Our sandwiches were eaten and I produced the three oranges, thinking it would be a treat for all. Instead I was cheerfully called down for packing excess. So I ate one and the other two returned to their hiding place, one in each leg of my riding britches that I wore underneath my corduroy skirt.

"Without the skirt I would have caused comment in Montana.

"Leaving our extra horses, we started again and rounded the knoll. We rode slowly, quietly. Dad remained on a pinnacle amidst a growth of young pines. Jim rode up close to me and whispered, 'You wait here and I'll ride the other side. When I put them up, they will come this way. When you hear them, you swing to the top and turn them towards home. I'll ride in—you follow them,' he said.

" 'Your job is to crowd them, stay right at their heels. Then I'll know where you are.'

"I nodded. He could depend on me. I waited and waited. My mare became uneasy. Nothing would keep her quiet, I thought. Quiet! I heard thunder. Ah ha! It was horses. Up over the top we went and headed for them. My mare was crazy to get in their midst. She flew when all at once I saw horses! horses! horses! headed right for me—coming as fast as they could, their heads up, manes flying, nostrils snorting forth moisture—like a stampede of steam engines, they came!

"I felt like I was in a handcar trying to escape a crack express about to overwhelm me when, magically, they turned.

A cloud of dust arose. In its midst I rode to crowd them. The faster I rode the less I saw. The dust cleared. Not a horse could be seen. Where were they? Where did they go? How could they get out of my sight? I rode in a circle again and again.

"They were gone.

"Bewildered, I stood still, exhausted from the fruitless search, blaming my stupid self for not letting the mare have her head. I looked again, half expecting to see them rise up from the earth. Then I settled myself to search each divide—along the top first, then the sweep around the valleys and up each draw. Ah! At last I saw them—just tiny forms of horses, all in single file going along at an easy full gallop. Jim was in the rear.

"I stood and watched them while they ran twenty miles or more up to the fork of a wishbone divide and back along the other side, never seeming to change their pace—mares, colts, old horses. I never thought horses could look so small. The air was so clear!

"They headed toward me and as I looked to the north I saw forbidden land—if they ever got over the ridge into that stretch so vast and rough, it would take weeks to find them. I was tired of fighting the uneasy creature I was riding, and as the horses came nearer she almost screamed to go, tossing her head and switching about.

"Suddenly I had lost sight of the horses again. The mare became frantic. I said to myself, 'You mean little horse, go run! If you want to, run your fool head off!' I gave her her head and away she flew like the wind and away from the direction I had seen the horses last—down, down the steepest, roughest country I ever saw. Down, coasting into space. Down to the bottom of nowhere.

"On she went, leaping over jagged rocks, brush and holes. At the bottom was a washout three feet deep and four feet wide. Into it she went—and out. With one scrambling leap, up she sprang to the top of a ridge covered with great shale rock, with now and then a jack pine or rotten stump breaking the smoothness of the path.

"It was shaped like the lid of a big sugar bowl but I was

hardly thinking of anything so sweet. Around the sugar bowl lid we flew. Had she made a misstep I would be going yet. Or maybe that North Pole aviator would have caught me on the fly.

"Then I looked up and right in front of me coming on the narrow trail was the wild bunch!

"The leader turned and like a squad of drilled soldiers, they swapped ends and were gone. Oh, what a sight! Unwittingly I had turned them precisely at the right moment. Now to crowd them. I certainly would not lose them this time. Around the ridge we flew—I thought I would yell to let Dad know where we were.

"Those horses left me like magic. Quickly my mare grabbed the bit and up she climbed, scrambling to the top of the divide, through a lot of jagged pines that had no soft brushing perfumed needles, only old broken branches that seemed to stick out without reason.

"Around I went, taking care not to leave any part of myself on a tree or rock, arriving in time to prevent them from going over the great beyond. My mare for the first time seemed choked for breath. I had not seen Jim all this time and I did not want to see him, knowing how badly I had disobeyed.

"Then suddenly, again—the horses!

"I yelled, 'Dad! Oh, Dad! Turn them! They're coming!'

"As calm as brushing ashes from a cigar, Dad moved his horse out from behind a bush. The horses turned then toward home. Out across an open stretch of land they spread themselves like three winds and Dad rode out in the throng. But he gradually drew to the left. What a picture he made—75 years old—six feet two—riding like a Centaur. A masterful mind and a light hand riding as smooth as a jockey.

"Wondering where Jim was, we rode on 'til they all got bunched again. It was amazing how colts, only a few days old, stayed right alongside their mothers. The horses singled out until they were a long string on one trail.

" 'We want to check them,' Dad said.

"How?"

" 'Just fall back easy. We have got them out of the rough country, now. Jim has gone to change horses again and bring up the relays. You go help him.'

"Where?"

"There!" He pointed to the corral. If ever I had a surprise it was to see that stone house looking right at me from its hidden group of pines. I would have sworn it was at least ten miles away. As I rode to Jim, it was plain my horse wanted no part of going home.

"He was on his own range, now, and it was hard to change his mind. After quite a bit of maneuvering on my part, Jim rode up to him, put his hand between his eyes and talked to him like a child, with a lot of kind, soothing words—kinder than any he spoke to me that day. I wished I was the horse. The animal moved his jaws as if chewing on something. And then one ear turned. It seemed hours but it was time well spent. With a gentle stroke, Jim rode away and left him.

"My horse looked all around, took a deep breath and exhaled with a sigh as if to say, 'Well, why didn't you say so in the first place?' He stood motionless a moment, then taking a last look, slowly started the way Jim was going. He followed until he sighted the wild bunch. Then with a snort he galloped to join them. There was no playing, now.

"My job was to crowd them. I must not let you forget that—doing it was another thing, for all I could see was a cloud of dust. Then Jim was gone and Dad disappeared after him.

"My mare was going just as fast as she could, yet I was standing still. Everything looked so far away. Why was I trying to catch up to this something that had vanished? I concluded it was useless to run my mare to death.

"I started to pull up and abandon the chase. Do you think I had anything to say? The insulted creature gave me one shrug as if to say, 'Stay on and keep quiet or get off and walk! I'll get there if you will give me a chance!' The dust cloud disappeared. We were coming to more washouts, divides and ravines. Having covered this spot at full speed with nothing in sight, everything went wrong. Not so easy in a rocky gully. I was tired. Exhausted. My tongue was swol-

35

len. My mouth painfully dry. The spent puffing breaths of my mare only added to my discomfort.

"Glad I was that I had no excess. The two oranges had been eaten and I had foolishly thrown the skins away. Tobacco was the only remedy after all and I did not have any. Believe me, I would have chewed skunk cabbage! Anything to relieve that dryness! Let me tell you the one way to tell a real cowhand is not to look at his boots or his hat, look at his lips. All the fine fixings or years of high polish will never erase those creases in the lips, which are so dry, so puffed, the outer skin has broken open.

"But your imagination leads you to a spring and you just keep on stretching that imagination until it snaps, finding yourself hell-on with the wild bunch again. They stood waiting. It was the surprise of my life. I did not understand until I saw barbed wire back of them and to the left of them. To the right was a drop-off to the valley below.

"I had been particularly cautioned not to crowd them when they got inside the wire. But now the fatal mistake. A woman's curiosity. Up to this moment, I had felt *some* pride for the fact that I had at least *tried* to help. Now they stood. All of them. My dreams of the wild horses were true, just as I had always pictured them. There were the large sweeping tails that touched the ground and the manes that came down to their knees.

"They were standing broadside now but their heads were turned towards me and their tails up. A beautiful black stepped forth with proud fighting air. He stood erect, head and tail nearly touching and he let out a snort that frightened my mare. And another snort. Then the rest joined in, one after another. Closely I examined them as they stood and I gloated upon the sight. Oh, they are too beautiful to be captured, broken, worked and sold to suffer and die. I must see them closer. Oh, so gradually I crept closer to them. At the end of the line was a big black greyhound type, marred with scars of ancient battles.

"He walked nervously back and forth—short paces only—as much as to say, 'Let us get out of here!' Not having seen Jim all this time I wanted to let him know where the horses

36

were so I thought one yell would tell everything.

"It did.

"It was the end. Like a flash they were gone.

"The only sound—and one that told a terrible tale—was the humming of the barbed wire that seemed to stand in the air and whip the everlasting thrums to the end of miles of fence. Its moans and screeches still play in my mind. I was done. The terrible feeling of what had happened to those wonderful horses—cut, bleeding, worthless—oh, the horror of it!

"It was to me the most dastardly thing ever done. Why did not I stand still and keep quiet? I will never forgive myself nor ask to be forgiven. Alone and lost, no horses, I could not move. My mare was tired. She made no effort to want to follow. I died a thousand deaths and suffered for each bleeding horse. Awakened from my sorrow, I heard Jim's voice.

"Which way did they go?"

"I just pointed.

"You wait here 'til I bring them back. Don't let them get down there!"

"I waited and waited, looking over the ridge where Jim had pointed. After long debate—duty or water—I chose water. I said to myself, 'It isn't fair. I won't take long.' Dimples was pleased, too.

"The instant we returned, Jim came through the fallen fence.

"Where did they go!" he cried.

"I thought he was out of his head. I had not heard or seen any horses.

"Where were you? he asked, as he galloped by on the road, leaving me like nothing. Sure enough, I felt like nothing. Then Dimples made up her mind it was time to leave and off she started. I looked over the edge of nowhere. I got to where they had left the earth. Jim went riding toward a divide far out to my right and Dad was riding the ridge far to the left.

"Jim motioned for me to go down. Once again I felt hopeful to think Jim trusted me with another duty. I certainly was not going to make any more mistakes. Down, down and around a tiny hidden foot trail—perfect under foot—but overhead a grassy wood and brush of all kinds—some with beautiful leafy boughs with thorns projecting an inch or more.

"They would stab you most gracefully. I put my nose into my elbow like a wedge and ducked. Once past this thicket, it opened to rocky going—nothing but the sharpest rocks projecting from every angle. Up and down we went and over wide open places that the water had made coming down from the hill.

"Broad jumps had to be made. No chance to go down and around except to go back and over the divide. It is still a mystery how the colts ever made it, when it was all a full grown horse could do.

"In front of the horses, a small divide loomed up. Jim and Dad were miles away, I just knew. The horses came to the fork. The leaders went left. I knew home was that direction, but when I looked again, the line was broken. Half went to the right. By this time I was on a high plateau looking down on them. As I got to the jumping off place, I heard Jim's voice speaking very gently, 'Turn them, Dell.'

"I looked at him hopelessly. To turn them simply couldn't be done.

"'Turn them!' came the command. No sweet kind words. No medals or loving cups for what I had already done. I was lucky to be alive. Every second meant the critical moment. Down we jumped. This was the steepest grade yet. I grabbed the saddle horn and hung on. I knew it would be fatal if my mount should fall. I would simply be thrown under her. No chance of going free of the horse. On the way down I heard Jim cackle.

"'What are you holding on to, Dell?'

"Mad? I could have killed him every jump, but I simply would not let go of that saddle horn. And when the mare would clear a huge boulder with her nose down to the ground like a hound, I would find myself riding with my arm clear up into my elbow. But I got there, and this time the credit was mine for turning them back.

"I was no longer a tenderfoot. It seemed that a horse could go anywhere, do anything. I gloried in Dimples' gameness.

She was like a new animal. She enjoyed the chase with fire and spirit. She never tired. On we galloped and I noticed they were coming to another check. Gradually they were dropping off. How careful and skillful they were, even in their untamed wilderness!

"I was right behind them close, and one by one they would drop out of sight. I wasn't going to crowd them any faster. I certainly was not going to push all these horses to their death.

"And then a puffing horse and a growling man rode up from the rear.

"Push them off! Crowd them off! Get up to them!"

"Well now that was the last straw! I was doing what I thought was *right,* this time!

"Don't you see them? There they go, down the valley two miles ahead! These here are the gentle bunch. We don't want them!"

"I looked down the valley and like a miniature I saw the wild bunch. Down out of sight Jim dropped. Now this dropping out of sight may not seem possible. But when your partner descends below to nowhere, and you hear crashing sounds a hundred feet below, and see nothing with both eyes open and in perfectly good daylight—you just know that he went. And you know there is no time to make your brain heavy with worry over what might have happened.

"Do it and find out! Dimples gave me no time for thought.

"Down *we* dropped from one rock to another and around a winding way. *Never* could we have gone back. At the end of the descent I noticed Jim motion to something on the side of the trail. I looked with strained eyes. There stood a three-year-old hiding behind a bush motionless as a deer. Scaring her out of her hiding place, she scrambled to the top of the divide. She was free, but when we got to the end of the draw, Dad headed the pretty thing into the bunch again.

"That was why Dad was riding that ridge—just to keep the strays and the bunch-quitters headed toward the pack. I called him an old fox. But I had commenced to wish that they would all get away and be free. The sport was in the chase.

39

"Of all the sports on horseback. never had I experienced anything so thrilling. I would like to say right here that these horses had been chased by every good stock man in the country because a horse without a brand, after he is a year old and not running with his mammy, is yours if you can get him. So they were 'manwise' as well as wild. They knew every trail to best a man and to hide out was one of their secrets.

"Jim announced we were going to get some water at the first ranch. Carefully we worked the bunch into a corner and through an open gateway into a pasture of some 350 acres, well fenced.

"Dad's trusty re-mount was as anxious to get home as the wild bunch was to return to the mountains. But in their bewildered state of mind, coming upon new territory, they sought a leader that would quiet them. And as Dad's old horse, gently without rushing, led the way seemingly unnoticed, they followed, going along the fence line and gradually slowing to a walk.

"Dell, you hold them until we return. Don't let them get back to that corner!"

"All right," I answered.

"I tagged along slowly at a walk, being careful not even to sneeze. Carefully stepping over holes, I noticed it was an old prairie dog town. The grass had grown over and it was difficult even to see the holes at a glance. I thought of the sad tales of stampedes and deaths of horses and riders because of a prairie dog hole. And here there were hundreds of them for a half-mile stretch. A rumble of hooves made me look up. They were coming like mad.

"Their ears lay back on their necks. They were fully determined to make the open gateway—the corner. Like a flash I wheeled and with the greatest speed yet, made my mare go. Running, leaping, we made the corner, headed them back, and not a horse touched the wire. As my demise did not occur in that mad relay, a great love grew in my heart for the horse and to this day there is nothing that can interfere with or alter that love.

"I can see now why King Richard III would give a kingdom for a horse!

"I went to the nearby ranch house as Dad and Jim stood guard. Order at last. The lady dropped a small bucket down a cistern and with a jerk the bucket dipped and was filled. As it neared the top I noticed live beasties in it. Lively little fellows. But the water was cold and while drinking, I strained it between my teeth, taking pains not to swallow the little swimmers. I know not if they were mosquitos or young frogs. The lady said it was snow water preserved for the summer supply.

"Mounted and on our way, it was now my turn to lead the wild horses the most direct way home. The point was to lead far enough ahead so they would not notice a rider, but would assume they were following another horse. To keep the right pace and go the right direction kept me busy. Often I would turn for advice from Jim, which was given by the wave of a hand.

"On we went over a great stretch of flat country toward the west edge of the Deercreek Mountains. Right on the edge, Slim threw up his tail, gave Jim a glance and dashed out of the bunch. He climbed the rugged banks and half way up he stopped, gave one snort and said good-bye. He lifted his mane and was gone.

"Jim said, 'Let him go. We'll get him later!'

"I do not know if he meant the same day or a month later. It proved a month. On we went. Somehow I found myself in the rear again when I ran into a big yearling that was all in. It had just quit. I did everything to make him move except Jim's baby talk. I did not feel so inclined. I took down my rope and made an easy headstall. The minute I tightened that rope I thought he would kill both Dimples and myself. I never saw such a fighting thing. He would strike like a bobcat and clash his teeth. Carefully I took off my rope and decided he could be captured.

"Also later.

"We were in a different kind of country by this time and it was chopped up into little bunches of plateaus and ravines, short scrubby pines, lots of sand rock formations, gullies and hills with more grass. After much effort I caught up with the bunch.

41

"To lead them was my job again.

"Which way?" I asked hopelessly.

"Follow the sun!" was Jim's quick answer.

"Out of the chopped up country I found myself on a road that led between two fences. Only five more miles to go. I could see Tongue River and for the first time I knew precisely where I was.

"Two lovely pines were landmarks. They stood along side one another like brother and sister in deep sorrow. The roadbed was hard. My Dimples' feet sounded like pistol shots. The noise of the herd behind sounded like the incessant sharp crackling of rapid fire rifles. Looking back, all I could see was a dark mass framed in a cloud of dust. The last long stretch was playing on my mare's wind but it would not be long now.

"Just another mile. I gave her all the rest I could, never putting an ounce of weight in the saddle if I could help it.

"The gate—the eventful gate—that could tell many tales. I rode past the opening about a hundred feet and waited. Dad bounded around a knoll to prevent their escape from that point. East of the gate was a group of knolls. At the foot of them was a network of washouts, but I saw Dad's old Bob horse take the lead and these snorting, sniffing and trembling creatures gingerly begin to go through the gate.

"I sighed with relief.

"But all at once I looked up. Then the cook at the ranch with arms pointing and white apron flying, hollared at the top of his lungs that the herd had arrived! The horses turned and came toward me! Jim was too far away and Dad was not in position to lead them so it was the race of my life. I was gaining when the big black (that uneasy one with the scars and barbed wire scratches) screamed past me.

"Like a cloudburst they all came. I meant nothing now——only another horse with a heavy load. I was furious and sick. The whole day meant nothing. They were free again. I could not turn them nor stop the stampede of those thundering feet. The great dust clouds choked me. Flying chunks of dirt hit me in the face. My legs were rubbing against those wild creatures.

"The leaping of my mare as she came to a washout had me nearly crazy. Horses behind me, to the right, to the left, in front of me. I heard a groan and a squeal like a flash. I saw a pair of heels go in the air followed by a snapping tail. Next I looked down and as Dimples was leaping this washout I saw a horse scrambling. This cleared my brain. I determined to stop, horses or no horses. I was not going to bite the dust and with all my might and will I managed to stop only to find after the horses had passed that there were no more washouts.

"In the very same instant I saw the horses and then Jim coming back toward me. Back over the washouts I led them—over we flew. My, such jumps ánd such crumbling banks! On we went through the gates. I saw Dad smile. Dad's old Bob horse ran up and greeted them as if to say, 'What happened? This is my home and there are lots of good things here for you.' "

Before rolling movie cameras in Los Angeles, Adele is shown in a scene from a silent western where she had to depend as much on her gun as her horse. This was before the technology of lighting and indoor studios. All scenes were shot outdoors, often rain or shine. When "killed" by gunfire in a scene in pouring rain, she frequently fell on other "corpses" to escape the mud puddles.

CHAPTER 3

THEY CAME TO NORTH OLMSTED

In 1908, critics' disenchantment, like the hard, hot sun, was setting fast on the once stellar attraction, the wild west show. Adele and Jimmy Parker, for their second season, were performing dangerous horse tricks with Colonel Cody's traveling entourage. In town after town, the murderous power of the press awaited the old Indian fighter and his hundred or so troupers and cavalry.

In Spokane, Washington, the *Spokesman Review* played an important role in the impending death of the most totally American spectator entertainment.

Its weapon was words:

BUFFALO BILL SHOW DISAPPOINTS!
Tent Not Filled and Many Spectators Leave During Performance
NOISE AND DUST FEATURES
Only One Redeeming Number on Entire Program
TRAIN HOLDUP AWFUL FROST

"When the bang of firearms let up and the smoke and dust had cleared sufficiently to permit the adjournment of Buffalo Bill's Congress of Rough Riders yesterday afternoon at Recreation Park, those of the spectators who remained in the big open-faced tent until the finish seemed to be of the belief that the Wild West Show was not all they had expected. About one-fourth of the seats were unoccupied when the show was underway and many more were vacant before the finish.

"The attendance last night was slightly in excess of that of the afternoon. On account of the miserably poor illumination, the night crowd was at a disadvantage. Many left.

"The regular performances were followed by a concert at which, the barkers proclaimed, would be presented a galaxy of entirely new vaudeville features. The concerts were fairly well patronized and those who attended were treated to a program of a few new things and some good things. The general verdict was that the good things were not new and the new ones not good.

One Good Thing On Program

"Aside from the exhibition of 3 fine horses with well-developed terpsichorean talent, there was nothing particularly worth seeing or mentioning on the program.

"As a Congress of Rough Riders it was not a special session. While the bronco busters might have made good with the real thing in the line of cavorting cayuses, the animals that figured in the busting business were not there with proper elasticity of vertebrae. The only horse in the lot that showed up with anything like the required spinal temblers was a mule. Even that animal would be an easy mark for the average unprofessional rough rider in the sagebrush nations.

"A football game on horseback between Indians and cowboys was a novelty that furnished amusement for a time, but what there was unique about it was chiefly the size of the monstor inflated bag with which the game was played. It was drawn out to such an interminable length that several hundred wearied ones started to make their exit during the progress of the game and they kept going regardless of the advice of the ushers who shouted, 'Set down! The show ain't half over and the best part is to come yit!'

Plenty Of Noise On Hand

"The wild and wooly west as portrayed with Indian fighting, stage and train robberies was all that could be expected providing that not much was anticipated. There were plenty of painted and bedecked braves in the role of the aborigines, numerous soldiers to affect the rescue of the paleface maiden captives when the job was pointed out by Buffalo Bill and no end of blank ammunition to produce the needed noise. With that combination augmented by the dust kicked and the shrill battle yells of the blood-thirsty braves, something like a satisfactory semblance of realism was affected.

"Although a real live locomotive and express car figured in the robbery of a Union Pacific train by border outlaws headed by a bandit queen, the episode did not elicit even faint applause. One reason for this may be that the train robbery was pulled off away at the dressing room end of the tent which was so far off that the greater part of the crowd could not see how the job was done, but it is probable that the majority of the spectators had seen more exciting train robberies at the motion picture shows.

Buffalo Willie In Red Shirt

"Colonel William Cody was given a generous round of applause when he appeared in his capacity of Buffalo Bill to introduce his world's congress of rough riders. He added considerable color to the scene by wearing a fiery red shirt although his once raven locks are now whitened by the snows of many winters. They hang as far down his back as before and he is the Centaur in the saddle that he has ever been.

"In his exhibition of marksmanship which consisted of riding his charger at a gallop and breaking glass balls tossed high in the air by a riding Indian, the colonel made a good score, although he had to assist the vision of the shooting eye by wearing spectacles.

Show Too Far West

"It is undoubtedly the consensus of opinion of those who attended the Wild West Show that its itinerary should be confined to territory east of the Mississippi and the farther in that direction the better. Too many train robberies are pulled off in the wild west country at this stage of civilization in the west to warrant presenting a bogus affair as an amusement feature. And while the Indians are docile, the days of Indian fighting are still within the memory of many living oldtimers.

"Bronco busting of the character to get a rise out of a crowd ought to be more exciting than that which can be seen at any country fair. And that could be said of the exhibition put on by Buffalo Bill's busters. . ."

The unsigned Spokane columnist did not represent the full

jury of U.S. newsmen. Others, more deep-feeling and vision-ary, perhaps, saw in the Buffalo Bill troupe an authentic and honest expression of the nation—wild, bogus, exagger-ated, too loud, silly and pushy as it no doubt was. These also were attributes of America.

Excited as any ten-year-old child, Arthur Greene of the *Morning Oregonian* likewise bought a ticket, a bag of pop-corn, two balloons, and saw the show. He scouted a good seat high up in the bleachers where he best could observe the In-dian massacre and the football game.

That evening he returned to his office, sat down to his typewriter, and sadly but dutifully prophesied the death of the wild west show in America. He was gentle. He was kind. He was considered a fair man:

OLD WEST REVIVED... BUFFALO BILL SHOW BREATHES SPIRIT OF PLAINS... CROWDS FILL BIG TENTS... SPECTACULAR SHOOTING... BATTLE OF SUMMIT SPRINGS AND BUCKING DISPLAYS ARE FEATURED IN COLONEL

CODY'S EXHIBITION

by Arthur Greene

"The spirit of the Old West and the echo of an age that is as remote as the days when Peter led the church militant to the Crusades... This is the dominant idea that pervaded me and made many others like me sit in tent and watch the Buffalo Bill show which is here for 2 days, opening its en-gagement yesterday afternoon.

"The exhibition must be judged as a thing apart from the ordinary hippodrome. I was almost bored at times when the confection agents were most active and when the spieling of the spielers announced the concert which was to follow. All tented exhibitions have these things—the concert and other petty grafts—but it seemed almost a sacrilege to hear them intruded.

"This show has a peculiar significance. If nothing else it must be commended as a means for preserving a counterfeit presentment of a certain phase of American life that has past. The wild west has moved on with the march of events and Deadwood is today as commonplace and conventional as Lynn, Massachusetts. The cowboy has become as nearly extinct as the dodo, and the Indian of romance is at Carlisle or his Happy Hunting Ground.

"I punched cattle on the plains with the last of the Knights of the Old Regime. The wild west was going by so fast at that time no matter how spry you were you could not board it. And that was 10 years ago. Since then all the romance has gone out of the primitive west. The dear danger of being unwatched, deeds which have filled our annals with glorious history have become only an old man's tale.

"The unending conflict between the red and the white man has ended and will be known no more among contemporary chronicallers.

"I remembered these things yesterday and grasped at that show as the last straw. For after Bill Cody there will be no others. And Cody is growing old. Many, many times I have seen him come into the arena with his rough riders, and always heretofore he has been able to carry off the illusion of virility, the debonaire assumption of courageous youth.

"But this time there was a pathos in his assuming of the character with which he is identified through the last 40 or more years of American history. He looks and acts old. Yet it is not time for Bill Cody to retire or to draw the curtain on the last of the wild west.

"We have outlived it so far. It has become incongruous. And this knightly figure of the last of the scouts and the show he gives us have little to do with today. The new generation does not understand and there is no good purpose in forcing the issue. But I think it is right and proper for its historic value to state that Johnny Baker and Colonel Cody, too, for that matter, shoot as well as they did 10 years ago.

"The cowboys and bronco busters who learned their cunning in South Chicago do very well at the equestrian game, the Indians look as fierce and do their stunts well enough.

"It is a show worth seeing and the tent was filled at each performance yesterday, and as long as the tent is filled, there can be no serious complaint.

"The Battle of Summit Springs is a realistic affair. The

49

bucking exhibition is thrilling. The entire performance is filled with interesting and sensational features which appeal to a circus crowd.

"You will do well to go out today and say good-bye to gallant old Bill Cody and his gallant crew. Take the kids for conscience sake. And tell them to remember what they see. . ."

The end of the wild west show couldn't dampen the enthusiasm, the intense determination or the fun of Adele Parker. She attracted people of all ages in every city and town she traveled. Partly because of her skill, her stories, her entertainment. Hardly anybody could define it. They simply said, "There's just something *about* that woman!"

An early Parker protegee was Marguerite Gormar Poley of Canoga Park, California.

"I lived with Adele Parker from late 1928 until 1934," Marguerite remembers. "Prior to the Wall Street crash, she sent me on to play fairs with Gus Hornbrook's Cheyenne Days outfit in her place. From the very beginning, I stayed with Adele at the stockyards. Later when she, Jim, Winnona and I shifted gears out to the 'Parker's Ranch' in the little rural town of North Olmsted, I can recall so well sleeping in bare rooms on mattresses made of gunny sacks filled with straw.

"It was the Cheyenne Days show," Marguerite said, "that brought Adele to Cleveland, and when it re-grouped, she simply said, 'You go for me.' By then she considered herself a teacher of horsemanship, 'established and accepted.' Whereas she had received $100 a week from Hornbrook, I was happy to get $40, knowing well enough that nobody could replace Adele.

"Among the better known performers on the Hornbrook bill were Augie Gomez, a great roping performer (he could rope twelve or more with one loop), Jitney Wright of the Keith-Albee circuit—a dancer of the 'Wright and Dale' dancing team, a great bronc rider, too; Tony Moreno, a good all-around man for a wild west show; French, a son-of-a-bitchin' Canadian, mean as hell, a steer rider and cruel to horses.

"I hated his guts.

"There also were Hughie Tooman and his wife. She, too, was a well-known western performer. Hughie drove a chariot in the original silent *Ben Hur* movie. But in the act he threw knives at his wife on a big board, some dipped and burning. He pinned her to the board so she couldn't move. All that after drinking hard.

"Adele knew all the old time film cowboys and many actors: Ken Maynard, Will Rogers, Fred Stone, Pauline Fredericks, Doug Fairbanks. Once she rode a buckskin horse for Doug Fairbanks at a horse show in California, probably at a location in Griffith Park, and won first prize. Doug was so delighted he kept shouting, 'Buck won the prize! Buck won the prize!' and he said to Adele, 'You're a prince!' He kept turning cartwheels and somersaults, for Doug Fairbanks was an acrobat, too.

"When I went with Cheyenne Days," Marguerite said, "Adele drove me down for a tryout in Zanesville, Ohio, where the fair tour was to begin. I'll never forget how mad Adele was because the horses were in such lousy shape. Gus was scotch to the hilt, had pastured them on poor ground, and what with the long train journey, half of them were sick and most of them so weak it was unbelievable. That afternoon she made Hornbrook wish he'd never been born."

Jim Parker rolled into town while Adele was still signing up kids at the stockyards. He was still a wiley, bronc-riding man with a soft whistle that could mean trouble. But the tougher the horse, the better Jim liked it and the better he did with it.

Mrs. Parker went to yard president A.Z. Baker and told him she had a perfectly good husband and they might as well put him to work. Up to then she had been known as Adele von Ohl. After that they called her Mrs. Parker.

"Jim Parker?" a stranger asked. "VERY friendly. VERY friendly. A red-headed Irishman. Big smile. BEAUTIFUL RIDER! Usually slightly drunk. Red-faced. Every bit as good a showman as she was. Took more chances most of the time. EVERYBODY was fond of Jim!"

At times when she had trouble with barnhands making fools of themselves and falling down drunk in public, she'd

51

say, "Jim may have had trouble with the bottle but he always did it quietly and he went away somewheres to do it."

Years ago when I was a green kid riding with toes pointed out, she said, "Ya know, Jim could ride a horse—you couldn't see his toes and he'd ride *to* ya!"

When he left, there were no recriminations. He was just not discussed. He was there so spasmodically and then, finally, he just didn't come back. She should have known better, she once admitted to a confidant. He was too much of a gambler. He gave her rings. He gave her necklaces, only to wager them in a poker game and have some dark men pounding on her doors to claim their winnings.

Even then there was no bitterness.

"But he was a bronc rider, rough-string rider, native of the north!" everybody said. "EVERYBODY LIKED JIM PARKER!"

The years wore on. The stable hands figured, "Well, people are bound to be curious about Mr. Parker. EVERYBODY was curious about him and it got to be kind of a game. You'd go down and they'd say, "Oh, you should have been here *yesterday*. Mr. Parker was here!"

They'd do that every couple of years or so.

"Boy, you should have been here yesterday. . . you should have been here last week! Mr. Parker was here!"

I never saw him. I never heard a description of him. I haven't any idea what the man was like. But Ivan and Bill were constantly at it—"Oh, you should have been here *yesterday!*"

Jim Parker was, above all, a pro. He could soothe the most cantankerous outlaw. It was a funny thing. People would send for Jim. They'd say, "That horse is a killer! Don't go near him!" He'd go there and find the horse all tied up—chains and straps and everything, and Jim would just go in and bump against him—"Why ya poor old fella, they got ya all tied up. Why they done that for?"—and he'd yank all that stuff off. And people would stand around waitin' to see him get killed.

Jim talked animal talk. He was just another horse to them. He could go into a corral and edge his way around. He

52

wouldn't get kicked or bitten. They wouldn't hurt him. He'd walk right under 'em, bump against them, crawl out between their hind legs. Do anything.

"You never met her husband?" asked the former North Olmsted chief of police. "I met him some years ago. He came back to the ranch just once. He came back and he was really boiled. He chased 'em all out of the house. He had a couple of guns. Adele called me up from someplace. I went over there in the squad car with a couple of sergeants and some shotguns. He was there, all right. Nona and her were out in the wilderness somewhere.

"I found the brother Percy upstairs hiding in a closet. Jimmy was going to run the whole crew of 'em out. He was a tough hombre, now, don't think he wasn't. He was plenty tough—like the old typical cowpoke he was. When I walked in the house, right away he start givin' me a lot of lip and I told him, "Jimmy, you just happen to be in North Olmsted, Ohio—now, we don't do this out here.'

"Well, he didn't care about that. He was going to stay there, though Adele said he wasn't. She wanted him out. I said, 'Well, Jim, there's only one thing I gotta do. I'm going to take your guns and I'll give you til midnight tonight to get out of here. If you're not gone, I'll have to remove you.'

"With that, he backed part way up the stairs, lookin' straight at me, sizin' me up.

"Maybe you can take me, Jim boy," I said, trying to be calm as milk about it, "but I got two sergeants with shotguns right outside that door and the first shot you fire, they're going to tear you down."

"Jeez! I thought he'd really explode then, but he didn't. He came forward down the stairs and handed over his guns. He came up that night about six o'clock.

"Can I have my guns?"

"I emptied the bullets and threw 'em in a drawer. I said, 'Sure can.'

"He went on about his business and never was seen here again."

"What I think happened then," the sergeant added, "was Jim went along like the rest of these floaters and just died

53

and is buried someplace in Potter's Field, maybe in Ohio, maybe in Pennsylvania. Indiana, maybe. That's what I think happened. . ."

When Adele Parker first stepped off the train to find her Cleveland booking cancelled, her keen sensitivity for publicity rose to the fore like cream in a bottle. Calling the *Cleveland Press* city desk from a pay booth, Mrs. Parker asked "if anyone over there had ever seen a rabbit drink a chocolate soda?" 'Dear Editor' columnist Charlotte Dixon hadn't, which is why the following appeared in the society column the next afternoon:

> *Giant Rabbit Found In Mall Drugstore; Eats Chocolate Sodas Plenty Fast; His Owner Says He Is a Dandy Pet—Never Barking, Mewing Or anything Except Little Sympathetic Noises; But Reporter Prefers Canaries.*

"Well, when you told me there was a famished giant hare—that is, a rabbit—eating ice cream sodas in the Mall Pharmacy in the Auditorium Hotel, I decided that you'd gone crazy on us and I suggested that you have a doctor look at your adenoids.

"But just then I got a tremendous taste for a soda and so I went over to the drugstore you mentioned and sure enough there was a rabbit and he was eating a chocolate soda so fast that it was all gone by the time I got my equilibrium back.

"Come to find out his name is Poncho and he will be two years old this coming March, so you see it's a regular old March hare. Furthermore he is healthy and chubby and his fur coat looks like the lining of a glove, and it made me think that maybe the beaver cap that Daniel Boone always wears in his pictures was made from a cousin of Poncho's

"I, of course, got all this information from Mrs. Adele von Ohl Parker, who claims a rabbit is the dearest kind of pet, although she has many others, especially horses. She is quite convinced when she says Poncho can't be surpassed as a pet for he doesn't bark or mew or gurgle or anything else except occasionally he gives a little 'uh-uh,' a sympathetic sort of grunt, and that's not at all annoying. . ."

The press had gamely struck at Mrs. Parker's "lure" for exposure and her uncanny power to attract reporters did not diminish while she lived. Great gobs of her advertising was accomplished by news stories which she "thought up." The city papers knew it and simply chuckled.

She was readership a la mode.

Seeing one shy reporter standing meekly in the drive was enough to entice her to top her best dramatic performance on the New Jersey stage.

"What do I wish, sir?" she would weep, covering her tear-stained countenance with both hands. "I will be realizing my life's dearest hope (cough, sob) to bring back the training of saddle horse and rider (sob, blowing of nose) to all who would know the feel of a slack bridle, horses, the white hill roads and streams that sing, and saddle leather fragrant in the sun. . ."

Once even the barnhands applauded.

Stranded flat in Cleveland with an incredible act but no place to play it, Adele managed to talk A.Z. Baker, manager of the Cleveland Stockyards, into giving an exhibition. Nobody had every heard of paying Depression money for that type of thing. Nobody, at least, down at the stockyards.

She had some horses wintering at Toledo and finally struck up a bargain with Baker.

"I asked him to ship the horses from Toledo and let me hang out my shingle at the show. It was a card tacked up: 'THOSE INTERESTED IN THE VON OHL SCHOOL OF HORSEMANSHIP PLEASE SIGN.'

"All those interested," she chuckled. "I was in business."

When she finished her exhibitions the card had six signatures. Most of them were barely legible, written by small boys who spent their time hanging around the yard. They were a wild bunch. Only one of them could pay her anything. He signed up for fifty-two weeks at a dollar a week for a half hour's instruction. He never got his full fifty-two lessons nor paid for many of the ones he did get. Some years later he went to Paris and took blues at the International Horse Show.

When Adele asked Baker to put glass in the windows and

to help fix up the place, it was the last straw. He pointed to the tons of broken glass in the yard and told her the local kids would have a real time with *new* glass.

"Let me handle the kids," she said. "All you have to do is put in the glass." Working together, the ring at the stockyards was fixed up. They put in new glass and hosed out an old feed room to make a combination tack and club room. Advertising was out of the question. Even if they had had some money to spend, it was bad taste to ask people to come to the stockyards to ride horses.

They smuggled customers in.

"They never knew where they were going until they got there," Mrs. Parker said with a grin. "It was cold that December. The riding hours were from nine in the evening until three a.m. We got some oil drums and built fires in them and brought in food. We fed the people. We fed them with the money we took in."

More and more people came to ride and eat. Parents bought horses for their children and some bought for themselves. A lot of boarders showed up and the Cleveland horsey bunch, barring parts of the snooty East Side, flourished in the stockyards. Baker bought a horse and signed up for polo lessons and later became a ten goal indoor player.

One afternoon they told Mrs. Parker thirty people were coming for lessons. She still had only two horses fit to teach on. How many could she handle they wanted to know. She told them to bring all thirty.

"That was my meat," she said.

Before long the neighborhood came to check up on the new windows. Mrs. Parker got out to meet them before the first rock was thrown. She took them in and put them to work.

"I made grooms and riders out of them," she said, "and taught them to go out and meet the public and take care of customers. Instead of breaking windows they picked up the broken glass in the yard. A bushel of broken glass bought a ride. They were my friends, my helpers and my workers. Tough little devils," she smiled. "I made three good jockeys and a trainer from that bunch."

They brought in a string of school horses from Chicago.

Anyone who came to the yard had to get on a horse. When they got on, they went to Mrs. Parker to find out what to do with themselves.

"That's how we got along without advertising," she said.

The Parkers opened their North Olmsted "ranch" in 1929 with two horses, one hundred and fifty dollars, and a small percentage of the business she had inspired at the yards.

"I was interested in developing riders," she said, "not in making dollars. I was on the outs with some of the people because of that. One man swore he would move in next door and break me. I told him that wouldn't be necessary, I'd always been broke anyway."

With her was her sister, Winnona, a fine horsewoman, and Jim.

"I had a bed and a chest of drawers," she recalled. "We borrowed horses here and there and the students brought food. We cooked it on a kerosene stove and drew our water at the pump. People dropped in and left things. A table or a chair, or something like that, and we got the house furnished. Since then," she said, "every other wish I ever had has been granted me. Even down to a clothes hamper."

When Mrs. Parker opened the door of the ranch, it stayed open. Good people did not own keys. There was a place by the fire for anyone who had a story to tell or time to listen to one. The good word of "stay on, stranger," wasn't dead on Mastick Road.

A friend remembered, "We all rode in here together that first day. How we longed to ride in that valley! I remember Jim Parker saying, 'Well, what'll we call this place?' I said, 'Why don't you call it a ranch?' The thing of it was, she had no money. She had to owe! owe! owe! Every place she turned, she owed somebody. A skip and a jump tryin' to make ends meet. At first out here, she wasn't too well known and not well liked, mostly because of her shy bankroll. It was a time when nobody had money—and money was the only thing talkin'. . .

"They figured her for a sucker at the start. She couldn't pay her bills. But that isn't cause to turn a body down. When you're trying to put two and two together, why put you down as a dog? She was trying her darndest in my opinion. At the beginning the whole bunch around here figured she was just a clump trying to get something for nothing. She was trying—that's my idea—she was trying her heart out. It was a hard start."

CHAPTER 4

A LITTLE TRUMPET, A LITTLE SHOW

"Sometimes, the neuro-surgeon said, "she was her own veterinarian and the horse simply would lie there on its side all bloated and puffing, in terrible shape. She'd pull up her sleeves, wash her hands, and stick one of them up its rectum, pulling out whatever she could get. She'd hear a snickering and turn around at us kids—'Get out of here! GET OUT of here!' It wasn't meant as a public thing."

There were thousands of unwritten rules. When she or any instructor was in trouble with a horse, you didn't rush in and give a hand—oh, no! She'd probably knock you down! It was HER problem—HER trouble. You would not offer. You stayed away, or did insult to her ability.

I saw her put an animal away once. Eagle. It broke her heart. This great big animal. She took him out back and put a cross on him from his eyes to his nose and hit the middle of the cross with pistol fire, and it was the only time I ever saw her weep. Another person spoke of her shooting another favorite that had been struck by a car. She went right out in the street and talked to the horse as if it were a wounded little dog. It put its long head confidingly in her hands as if to help her draw the dreaded cross with a piece of chalk.

Other times we'd go running into the house yelling, "Mrs. Parker! Mrs. Parker! So-and-so hasn't eaten his grain! Big deal. She'd come stomping out and go in to *talk* to the horse. She'd say, "Now, just what is the trouble with you? Why haven't you eaten? Is there something worrying you?" Then she'd say, "Oh, you think it doesn't taste good? Well, I'll taste it for you." She'd take up a small handful, pop it into her mouth and say, "Too salty! Take it out and give it to Fred!"

Mrs. Parker could take a stallion down that valley road and she'd talk to him and he'd be a baby. She could take the big black stallion down the valley road and meet mares and he'd never touch 'em. Wouldn't look at 'em, even. Walk right past 'em. And that is something. . .

And if she went to a friend's home for an evening, she'd insist on sleeping on the floor by her saddle, with a little blanket over her. And she'd make us kids sleep on the couch. She broke bread at many tables. She was universally liked. Almost. They all could find flaws, of course—in the way she did things, the way she lived. But she was solid as the stable floor.

Her identification with animals was handed down a thousand times over. Millie's horse, Little Mountain, one time suffered an impaction. The doctor had medicated the animal and it could not pass anything for two weeks. They had nearly given up, suffering with the horse day and night, giving him enemas, etc. Millie was dying with the horse for a fact. Finally after some weeks of this and no movement of the animal's bowels, Dr. Fuller came in and said, "How is it going today, Millie?"

"Oh," she cried, her eyes full of tears, "we just had the most wonderful bowel movement!"

Mrs. Parker's "sixth sense" with dumb animals and particularly horses was legend since her girlhood.

"Sure," her blacksmith Walter Page conceded, "if a horse were difficult to control, she'd take advantage of the situation. If a horse had a tendency to rear or plunge to the barn, she would take and actually put this in the form of a command. She would teach him to get *better* at it. Then she'd take him *away* from the barn and do the same thing.

"I was schooled in a field of horsemanship pretty foreign to this country," Page said. "A lot of rough horses—different from this domestic stuff. Yet I cannot—simply cannot—do many of the things Mrs. Parker did. Nobody around here can do them. Oh, we can be more regimented and concise. But she could *get out* of a horse. Certainly you give a verbal command, you do something to get to him physically. You condition his reflexes. This is true.

"But she could *so subtly* condition his reflexes—this is the thing. There is a point of telepathy with a horse. Absolutely. A horse's *awareness* of you. She had this ability to associate and communicate. Some people talk about a little aid; you drop a leg, you check and you collect. There's *got* to be something more than physical. If you want to learn this, walk into a corral full of broncs. I've got a gelding right back there now—I've roped steers off him for years—I know what he can do. But if I'm not mentally right on a given morning, if I'm not emotionally set to tackle him, I turn him loose. I don't mess with him.

"Anyway," said Walter Page, "what is so profound about telepathy between horse and rider? It's easily recognizable between people. Many times we are capable of detecting an 'honest person,' for example. He don't have to say, 'Well, here, I'm honest.' A lot of times we can detect the extremely deceptive person when he says the same thing the honest fellow said. This is accepted as true in human relationships. It's easier to understand the animal.

"Still," he added, "I wouldn't have wanted to ride a horse she had broken because she *never broke them,* and that would worry the hell out of me! I mean, 'Whe-e-e-e-e! So he wants to buck half a mile!' There was something wonderful in that.

"Many would-be horsemen try to grasp the spirit of the thing with paraphernalia—you can't do this. You can't physically implement a motive. You take a person with a given motive and impetus to do something. He can take half of what you got and get it done. You can have all of the tools. If you lack impetus, if you lack *motive,* you're out of it. Some attack riding by collecting the right bridles and saddles and the right barn and stable.

"It goes beyond that. Persons resented Adele because she had something they just couldn't grasp or buy with money. When she said there was a communication, she was right. As I say, I've turned horses loose before. I've walked into a corral and if I felt out of sorts, if I wasn't right upstairs, I'd turn the animal loose.

"She had her old clowns on that place," the blacksmith Walter Page added, "and this I didn't like, nor could I understand it. Why she would have those old cripples go out there stumble-bumming around, I could never comprehend—now THERE was a contradiction, a decided contradiction of her nature. She probably felt, 'Well, I've packed 'em for so many years. *I've* been hurtin, too. I've had my knees broke up. I've got to survive financially here, so go make a dollar or two.'

"It *might* have been her attitude. She *was* crippled up for years. Knees and all. *All* of her stock wasn't crippled. She had horses who'd be better off if they'd been a little sore——boy, they could buck and raise hell!"

Some of her horses were kickers. A classic Parker statement would be: "Stay away from that horse. He kicks. Now if he kicks your horse and breaks a leg, I got to shoot that horse. But if he breaks *your* leg, I don't care, we can put a cast on *you!*" She yelled to make headway with pupils and never altered that tone in the ring: "CHIN IN! DROP YOUR HEELS!"

Once, Mrs. Parker was perceptibly upset with a cantankerous stallion. A young high school girl ran to assist only to catch full force Mrs. Parker's biting admonition, "I TOLD YOU, NEVER BUY A HORSE WITH FOUR WHITE STOCKINGS!"

"Yes'm."

"That was the extent of it," the girl said later. *"It wasn't even my horse.* I don't know who it belonged to but it was a horse who had four white stockings and it was wide in the eyes and she added, 'NEVER BUY A HORSE THAT IS WIDE IN THE EYES!' and she continued to let me have it. I took a bawling out for a horse I didn't own. But you took her as she was. You liked her or you didn't and you adapted to the day."

It was a treat to watch Walter Page, blacksmith, pound his shoes, placing them cherry red in a keg of water. He had good brawny arms with which he lifted the horses feet, bending them into his leather apron, wet with sweat. He bent and sweat and hammered and talked of the fun of Adele von Ohl Parker.

"There was a team of mules that weren't broke," he said without glancing up. "They'd been goofed around with for years. And this old boy with the buffalo come through. Big strong man from the Dakotas. Now he had this cottin-pickin' buffalo broke—I mean like a *rein-horse!* This was great. Now who in hell *today* would keep a buffalo around? Well, she asks buffalo man if he'd like to drive them mules.

"As I say, they'd been dinked with for years. I had softened 'em up more than once. But they'd walk out of the barns and just leave out of the clear blue. Kids would turn 'em loose. They were pretty smart. He said, 'Oh yeah, he'd drive 'em.' Later he said, 'Geez, I took them two things up there in the barn and I strapped the harness on 'em and I stepped behind 'em to go and they just sold out flat. Full motor. Right out of the barn!'

"He said, 'By God, I fell on one ring to stop 'em. I just fell on one ring and spun around and got 'em stopped. Then I proceeded to drive 'em. Hooked 'em up to an old buckboard.' He said them cottin-pickin' mules just put in gear out in that front pasture.

" 'By the time I was around the thing a dozen times there wasn't nothin' left of that thing the mules were tied to but the seat. The boards had shaken out and everything!' "

"She knew he was a horseman and she knew what would happen," blacksmith Walter Page chuckled, "She'd never do this with a kid. She'd never set a kid up. But the fellow *drove* them mules.

"Once she said, 'Walter, I want you to take this cow to town.'

"I said, 'No—why? Why do you want me to do this?' I didn't know it but the cow, Sybil, must have been in love with me, see? Now I had nothin' to do with Sybil. Maybe that's why she loved me. I went in the barn. I took ahold of Sybil. Had a halter on her. I walked her up the trailer. She follows me in that trailer. I tie her in. Flip up the gate. Adele says, 'Walter, you're the only man she's ever followed into a trailer!'

"By God, that's why she wanted me to go.

"So we go downtown and I'm walkin' down the street (I wasn't part of this, it was Mrs. Parker's bit, you know) and I'm aholdin' Sybil. And this bosomy model is walkin' along side, you know (I'd walked down the street with a girl before, but I never had a cow between us).

"This one reporter says, 'We *got* to caption this!' and I said, 'Just call it udder nonsense.' The reporter said he didn't get it but the model wondered if I meant the cow or her. Mrs. Parker had a way of getting you involved clear up to your navel in these things. Anyways I never saw a penny for the escapade. She did these things which you just sluffed off.

"And I remember," the blacksmith Walter Page said, "the winter day I came back from the coast. Coming up the drive I saw her about to step onto a horse. It'd been fifteen years anyway since I'd lived at the ranch as a kid. As if I had only returned from an errand of some few minutes, she said, 'Walter, how are you? I'm going to ride this horse.'

"Pretty nice big stallion."

"How would you like to ride him?"

"Fine."

"So I stepped on, slapped him on the butt and rode off, and he bowed up a little bit but I just ignored it. We rode out on the ring and jogged around—she standing there, taking it all in. She says, 'Lope him off, Walter!' and I loped him off. She had some jumps there. I was sittin' there stock saddle, see. I don't like to jump a horse in stock saddle. She said, 'Take him into one of them fences!' Fine. About three-foot fence. And I copped that and we loped around a little bit.

"She said, 'Take him over a few more!'

"I took him over a few more, jogged him around and came back. I said, 'Nice horse.' Well, he was a dirty side-winding dude, and what she wanted to do was see him come on wild. It would have tickled her to death if he'd of bucked me down, providing, of course, I lived. It didn't offend me. But I knew her enough to be suspicious.

"This amused me about her," said Walter Page. Comraderie, you know? I understood her. It was even a form of flattery, really. I laughed about it later, but it was a good deal later.

"The unstable factor," said the blacksmith, "was her lack of consistency. Take the horse out and she'd work him and school him. No question about it. She *knew how*. But she'd work him a week and lay up. Then she'd get very zestful over a show or a number of friends would show up for a good time. She'd jerk some old clown out and put him through his paces, ready or not.

"She'd do this. . .

"But she was no fake. Now, she wasn't. I've seen her ride—helluva job. She just wasn't controlled. Impulse! Impulse! That was the way she lived. Part of this freedom thing. Strangely, perhaps, her contempt for society predominated—yet she contributed to it. Old campers can laugh at the place nostalgically. It was one heck of a place. They were themselves there. Kids have a tendency to romanticize, to live in a semi-state of fantasy. And she permeated this spirit.

"As an adult I could see what it was—I mean *after all*. . .but you wouldn't disparage the kids. . ."

Walter Page took off his blue apron and scrubbed his big hands. "In one sense," he observed, "she was more real than what we casually consider acceptable and stable and sequential. The fact that she wasn't too consistent lent to her sincerity in some things. Some of her was definitely affectation—a hell of a lot of it wasn't."

"Did she know who she was?"

"I think she was always in control. She had a sense of humor. And I think she would go off on the theatrics *knowing* she was being theatrical. She was putting it on, putting it on. She was being facetious. Oh, no, that was a *thing!* The scenes on the driveway where an owner and horse were leaving against her will—this was clearly calculative.

"Oh, yes, this wasn't all of the sudden she had an awareness of what was—this was simply good *showmanship!* She wanted to retain the boarder. The individual. This cannot be construed in any way as an unknowing reaction to a condition.

"I was there as a kid. I worked for her," Walter Page recalled. "It wasn't a day camp or anything then. I took care of the upper barn, going to school from there. One time she got plum mad at me—I mean REAL mad. She threw me off but I wouldn't go. I wouldn't leave. That afternoon I went into dinner. She came over and scratched my head and said, 'All right, let's forget it now.'

"I was there two winters and a summer and then I was in

65

circuit with harness horses. Then I went to the service and was gone a long time. I came home and lived on the coast for ten years. I broke horses in Montana and all over the country. Then I came back here and shod horses. And I found my way back to Parker's Ranch. I really didn't want to shoe her string horses. I didn't want to have too much to do with the outfit because the conditions were so bad from a shoer's point of view.

"Flies all over the place. This is common in any barn, but my God, them string horses! I was reluctant to shoe them for I hated like heck to be rounding up somebody to shoe flies. But I did it. She couldn't get anybody else. I don't mean I martyred myself, but I did it reluctantly.

"There were a lot of diversified people there. The fact they were so diversified was an attraction to the place. There wasn't the affected atmosphere you find around the super-clean saddle-bred barn—stuff I have no use for.

"I mean I don't respond to that sort of thing. So this was good. This was attractive to people. All those different personalities coming in there. Some simply to ride a horse. Others merely to associate and be free. I mean just *relax* and go about their business. This was confusing to Mrs. Parker. I think Mrs. Parker would not have been as inconsistent as she was were it not for this influence.

"She wasn't only the proprietress of the place," Walter Page the blacksmith declared, "she was its victim. She had harassments. People were in her way by the very nature of the place.

"Fine people went in and out of there. I could point out persons around town who are the epitome of what we call socially acceptable intellectuals who were very much a part of the place, and who did not become as haphazard as she. I mean *very directed people*.

"I did my work," he added, "but she could have got along without me there. My God, she had able-bodied men who could do my job plumb easy. As I say, I'm not prejudiced in this. I'm not overly sentimental about Mrs. Parker. I can see through the fake, certainly, and the theatrics and the baloney. I tell you I could.

66

"It didn't dent her humanity.

"I can sum her up for you easy," said the blacksmith Walter Page. "Her class transcended the paraphernalia associated with class. She hardly required crutches or props. I look at her realistically. See, I think some people try to evaluate her from the standpoint of the perfect human being. Well, who in hell can you do *that* with?

"Looking at Adele Parker with as much respect as you would afford any other, acknowledging the fact that she was mortal and fallible, the conclusion was clear-cut.

"The woman had class.

"Not that she didn't make damn sure she asserted herself over any male," the blacksmith cautioned—"now I'm talkin' in a horse sense. I don't mean when it come to plumbing. In later years this mellowed. She got a little softer on male accomplishment with a horse. I recall her tryin' to flatter me to get me to do somethin' for her. I'd just kid her. I'd tell her she don't have to do that.

"If I have time, I'll do it. If I don't, I won't. Now come on, Mrs. Parker, if I was as good as you say, I'd *be* somethin'. Now cut it out. . ."

"I'd kid her, see?"

A friend once asked Mrs. Parker why she paid so much attention to some of the dusty relics that wheeze their way up her drive, instead of spending more time sizing up the expensive models. Mrs. Parker said the dusty ones look as if they have come a long way and might be going further. They have something to tell about where they have been and might need a little help to get where they are going. A lot of them stayed awhile. Some of them stayed just long enough to die among friends.

"Everyone needs a place to go," she said.

"I showed her my bright new car," her student proclaimed. "She said she didn't care for my new car as much as she did the old one. She said an old car had stature and a lot of tales to tell. And a new car was not very much. I suppose she valued things that were aged more because they had memory. . . and had known happiness. And by then, of course, she, too, was old.

"On a hot summer's evening sometimes there was such a gang there. Sometimes she'd bring out watermelon. She'd break it open. Everyone around. Or there'd be a group of children there and she'd say, 'Let's go up to the Dairy Queen. I'll treat! My treat! One night we went to get in the station wagon and she said, 'Oh, no. Let's take the old Hudson. I just love that car!'

"We piled into the Hudson and chug-chug-chugged to the Dairy Queen."

"She had an identity with the relics," assured the blacksmith Walter Page. "No alterior motives. She *used* them, you say? She might have had to pay somebody else a dollar an hour. All right, so she could keep an eye on a bum and pay him two dollars a week. I think there was some element of advantage for her. This wasn't exploiting. I've worked for guys who paid me so much an hour, and *boy!* They used hell out of me—made *sure* they used me. Far harder than she did.

"Sure, people complained of the ranch. She could have got help. A circus man came through there—a very good horse man. A colored fella came through there. A big strong man. An intelligent Negro. Called him 'Thirteen.' And he really took care of them horses. I mean he was really a go-gettin' kind of man. He spit and polished. But they couldn't stay. It was financially impossible. But them guys who came through there plumb broke—I mean absolutely sacked out—they'd be there long enough to get on their feet and find a decent job.

"She would continually remunerate in one form or another but I think they had the edge on her. I don't think she got the better of it. Maybe occasionally fifty-fifty.

"We all had our idiosyncracies," said the blacksmith Walter Page, "some more than usual. But one thing about her, she never judged you. If it was Frank's time to get drunk, Frank went and got drunk. Mrs. Parker never censored. She didn't condone, neither. She merely accepted it. I remember a few times when I was a kid.

"Well, Frank's down there so drunk I can't hardly hear him. I have to go get Frank.'

68

"Down the road she'd go in that station wagon. Pick up Frank. Bring him back. Put him to bed. He'd get sober, would be fine for another month or whatever the time lapse would be until he had to go again and manifest this desire for booze.

"This was a good thing in this woman.

"This was legitimate.

"Was she the epitome of no system? Of course," Walter Page concluded. "You can't draw disagreement there. Her girls attempted some notion of order and failed. And when gents came by with a whole new plan of operations, it was like taking sandpaper to their noses. It's like somebody saying to me, 'Why don't you get that horse gentle?' while it's tearin' my head off. She didn't want it too regimented—that's all! I could understand this. She didn't want cold economics to touch her. It was reality she vied with, recognizing it only to a point. The only reality she ever fully bowed to was death."

Certain of us *pleaded* with her to find a manager. We *had* one man! Perfect! Superb, in fact! But when we came out one day, he was gone. Somebody snuffed him away. Then we got Marty, the circus man. "Oh," he'd say, "if only I had some elephants. Don't know a thing about horses, though. I think I'll catch an elephant!" Remember John out there? Worked on the railroad. Really fantastic 'cause he didn't drink. And he was clean and pretty much preserved.

Then the girls and Mrs. Parker went to see businessman Karl Stats one sunshiny afternoon, putting the press on *him*.

"We sat and we talked," said Karl Stats. "One said, 'Well, now, what are you going to do if you go down to the barn and find that Bill hasn't fed the horses? What are you going to do if the barn isn't cleaned out?'

"I said, 'I'm going to tell him about it in no short order.'

"Well," she says, "supposin' tomorrow you come down and you see it again?"

"I says, 'Then he's *really* gonna get chewed out!'

"Well," she says, "supposin' the next day he doesn't do it? *Then* what are you gonna do?"

"I says, 'He's gonna be walkin' down the road right then!'

69

"Well, who's gonna feed the horses?"

"I said, 'If nothing else, I'm going to help and so are the rest of you. But we're not going to put up with this!' And I said, 'By the same token, if *you* don't do *your* jobs, *you're* going to walk down the road, too. If we decide out there this is what we're going to do and you got a job to do, you better do it, because if you don't do it, you're not going to be there, either. And this is the way it's got to be!'

"Of course Parker forgot the whole proposition. What Parker *really* wanted was simply someone to go out and clean the barns and feed the horses. That's *all* she was interested in. . . *not* in me runnin' that ranch. Now I tell you it was a place. . .

"She had an old horse out there one time that wasn't good for anything," Stats chuckled. "A fella come out and she tells him how wonderful this plug was. Then she commences to rent this piece of horsemeat for his private use for sixty-five dollars a month. If she could have gotten *thirty-five* dollars a month out of that mount, she'd have done very good. So in two month's time the fella got wise and walked off and she got nothing after that. This is where she never used good judgment. This guy didn't know what he was doin' so she took him.

"Another thing," he said. "She goes out and buys septic tanks and toilets. Now she's going to put in running toilets but she has no place to put 'em. No building to put 'em in. I re-wired all her barns down there. It's a wonder they didn't burn up the way the electricity was in. Yes, I felt sorry for her and I went down there and I re-wired 'em and fixed up some of her cars and things until I finally got wise and said, 'Look here, Stats, you'll work here the rest of your life. This is Mrs. Parker! And when you walk out, she'll get somebody else to help her.' This was her great knack."

"There were times," her counselors admitted, "that we got madder than hell at her. She'd do things we knew were detrimental to the business and her own interest. We'd say, 'Oh, why CAN'T we clean up this place? Why CAN'T we throw it out?'

"Well, you CAN—I *want* you to clean it up—but wait til I

get out there!"

"She would never let you go ahead and do it. It was the one thing that was very hard for her in everything—to ever COMPLETELY relinquish the reins to another person. She NEEDED to help, though often she would say, 'I just want you to take over and run this place—just—run it!'

"But if you said, 'Well, the first thing we'll do is move this over here—then we'll get rid of *that*. . .' about the time you got to the word 'rid' the jig was up.

"But you're not going to do THAT!"

"Well, we're going to change these horses—we *can't* continue with these. . ."

"OH, WELL! You're *not* going to get rid of so-and-so!"

"She had a gorgeous side saddle with velvet inserts that the rats had devoured in the top of the barn. And there were other saddles there, particularly a McClellan army saddle that had been broken for twenty years and couldn't be repaired and these were saved along with a mess of three-legged tables.

"Junk! Bits and pieces of anything would be saved and stored. We cleaned it out. I'll be damned—she got home—we were all waiting around for her to be happy and thrilled with the clean place. She stepped out of the car and found a buckle off one of those old pieces of leather. She shot sky high!

"When she calmed down, she just made more junk. It, too, piled up. Then she'd take it upon herself to clean the Geezle Barn and put everything *else* outside. It would be out there a month, in all kinds of weather. Then the Geezle Barn would be clean but all the rest would be swept into the garage where the chickens roosted and crapped on it, and one day, finally, an attack would be made on the garage and the stuff ended up outside and from there back to the Geezle Barn.

"Each time, more and more deterioration.

"But something always had a value, even if it simply brought back a memory.

"Those things all were going to be put to good use some day. So—no one dare touch anything. She knew PRECISELY what was out there. You had to FIGHT her to help her! You *did!*

71

"We did get the barn floor cleaned out once. She had that sleigh and a couple of Roman chariots in there. And saddles—some of them priceless. People even then were trying to get their hands on them. Where they did go later on, I can't tell you. Others not worth keeping. But someone would come by and say, 'Oh, *you can fix this up!* You can't *buy* leather like this anymore. It's a sturdy piece, all right!'

"Back it went."

The short-term mechanic we once highjacked for a week was sure the woman stood out in the road and waved in junk dealers. The barn was repaired with a spare board here, a piece of wood there. If the wind blew hard, we'd put up another. After awhile you exhausted the supply of useable old boards—they all were nailed to the barn. I went back there six years after we had cleaned the place. It was high as your head in old wood and rubbish. Rocks and bricks and asphalt and timbers. . . When she put things in a drawer, you never saw them again. She saved every chair, every rubberband, every everything she could find. If you had a box—"well, we can always put *this* in that box!"

"Sure," said the volunteer, "she needed wood to patch those stables. Horses were falling out of the stalls. Nevertheless, you were sure *this* time she meant it and so you killed yourself trying to help. From the house to the big barn to the shed to the Geezle Barn to the house—gathering more and more each revolution."

Countless numbers over so many years put in hard and diligent toil at Parker's. I'm not sure why, except for the joy of entering that other world for an hour or so. You did it and you didn't know why you were doing it. Some did so much for her and she didn't appreciate it. Then they stopped doing things.

They were out of her life.

What did Mrs. Parker give? I think Mrs. Parker gave nothing. She took. She took everything there was. Then again, she exposed one to her personality and the chance for running barefoot in its shadow. To the very end, children were still agog with the sparkling of a star, tarnished though it had become.

So all those who might well have proven capable business managers became completely disenchanted and frustrated and ultimately declared, "What's the use? There's no point in trying to make any improvement here. The way it is is the way it always has been and always will be until the end."

Her genius lay in other spheres.

Her whole notion of training is completely gone now. There are different breeds of horses coming along—but the "nice-ness" that she taught is gone, the niceness between rider and horse... the notion deep inside one that the animal is not just some machine of a thing you hop on and gallop off on on a Sunday afternoon.

Maybe I think this because I was there for so long and I lived with them. The average customer who came on Sunday would never see this—she was a character to those dreaded Sunday riders. An oddity. A comedian. But what she had, you don't find anymore. Kids in modern riding schools don't have it. There are lots of new stables. And for what owners want in horse show material, they'll produce it. But the dear little tricks of the trade are gone.

Her idea was simply to get the animal to do what she wanted it to do in the nicest way she could do it. She said it was just like dancing with a person. You ask the horse to come with you. That's all.

"She had," the blacksmith admitted, "a funny sense of values around critters. Value was personal association. Market and price secondary. God, she kept some horrible dogs around. A few good horses but she kept worthless baggage for years. Sentimental value. One horse in particular had a trait about him.

"I know the only reason she kept him was to use as a point of instruction with the kids. He was an ornery jughead to lead. One you had to watch. Just amazing some of those kids—*all* of 'em—learned to survive around a horse. I guarantee that. And they'd never done it around absolutely dead broke critters."

Phyllis Krueger, the Lakewood school teacher, fondly recalls Mac Donald's Jet.

"Listen, sweetie, that was when Eugenia and Mrs. Parker were out in Wyoming prancing about and I was in charge of the barn. Jet, the blind stud, was in the stall Flare was in, and they had this lovely saddle-bred mare—and we kept trying to breed her and nothing happened.

"Somehow she got loose during the night. She got out. It was a hot night and we left the top door of the stud stall ajar (he was blind and we figured nothing could excite him). But Roxy, the lovely mare, wasn't blind and she was cavorting all around. She was obviously tootling around there, her buttocks against the door. He probably was nipping her on the rump if the truth were known. And she kicked the latch up.

"What occurred then I don't know but the next morning the barn man came.

"Mrs. Krueger! You know that blind horse? He was loose but I put him back in his stall."

"Well, fine, thank you very much."

"In a few minutes he was back again.

"You know that mare? She's loose, too, and she's caught between the wagon and the corn crib. . ."

"We went out there and there was Roxie standing and she had hoof marks on her rump. Well, Mary and my daughter and I swore to secrecy. Whatever the gestation period is for horses. . . we counted on our fingers. Roxie, like a woman of the street, was sent back to her family. Not a convent."

Her blacksmith, Walter Page, was as cautious of Mrs. Parker's publicity as he was her sense of mischief.

"There was to be a publicity stunt for a motion picture," he recalled with a distinct sense of pain. "I was reluctant as usual about her deals. She said, nevertheless, 'I'd appreciate you and a few of the boys dressing up and taking the horses out here for a great promotion.'

"Of course we knew Mrs. Parker.

"No, thanks, we don't want to do this."

"She says, 'Just put on your best hat.'

"I said, 'I've only got one hat and it's none too good.'

"That's all right," she says, "go buy a new one. I'll pay for it."

"I looked at her and said, 'Well, ah, I don't really want a new one.'

"She said, 'Oh, *I insist*. I'll pay for it.'

"So I sent for a good hat. The hat cost me twenty dollars. So I got my good hat. I mean I wasn't anxious about this at all. Sure enough, everybody was ready and the deal fell through. It wasn't her fault. Well, I had my hat. She received some remuneration out of this. She was paid for her expense or inconvenience or whatever. She didn't again mention payin' for the hat. . ."

Karl Stats, the man who hung around and fixed things, is not likely to forget one Fourth of July Festival of Freedom in Cleveland Stadium.

"Parker and me tootled down to the Stadium with 32 horses, including two stallions and four mares in heat," chuckled Stats. "In spite of the fact one stallion broke loose with nothin' but love light in his eyes, we went onto the field at 8:23, right on schedule.

"The group I was with came in from left field with a covered wagon headed towards homeplate. Coming in the other direction were the Indians who were to meet us at the batter's box for a fight to the death. I never laughed so hard because the woman at the reins of the covered wagon was pregnant and was going to give birth any moment and here we were with three dozen horses in the midst of fighting Indians.

"The police had promised to bring some guns out to the ranch so that we could shoot 'em in front of these horses to get 'em used to the noise, but they forgot. So here we go in front of 50,000 people ready to shoot 38 caliber guns in front of these animals for the first time. You can imagine giving kids guns with blanks in them. They're gonna have a circus. When we hit homeplate and the shooting started, you'd have thought World War III had begun.

"My boy ended up in the third base dugout. His, miraculously, was the only pony that panicked."

Surely Mrs. Parker put a bit of excitement into the neighborhood. I've seen cows loose, running around the street. I woke up one morning and found a horse in the front yard. Once her cow had a calf under our porch.

One year the little Catholic church on W. 25th Street had worked hard on a nativity scene in its front yard. Two sisters approached Mrs. Parker for the loan of a few animals to touch up the display. They were there for a week. The nuns had a plaster cow and an asbestos angel or two. A few days later, a phone call.

"That pony of yours kicked the wings off the angel! And—and the mules are jumping over little Lord Jesus and they're chasing the sheep around and sashaying all over the yard down here!"

Somebody had to go down and restore order. Parker put a call in to the city desk. "I've got a headline for you," she wailed—"Mule Kicks Wings Off Angel."

"Certainly no complaints to speak of," the North Olmsted police lieutenant assured. "If we *had* a complaint, we went over to speak to her and she remedied it right away. No trouble at all. Why, the woman was a saint! She never got tough or anything like that. She'd always say, 'Certainly, lieutenant, if it's bothering those people, why I'll correct it!' So very nice that way. Some people thought she was, well, hard-boiled and crude, and—like that... Just the opposite. Just the opposite..."

Nevertheless her goats were insane. They'd climb on top of people's cars. It was average to glance out and see part of her herd standing on top of the car roofs eating the leaves off the trees. The woman wasn't concerned about the cars.

"Get those goats off! *They'll fall and hurt themselves!*"

Her neighbor, the plumber, had put in holly and flowering crabtree (a present to his wife on Mother's Day). Parker's goats ate up all of that—it was like a pretzel when they had consumed their fill. Then there were the boxwoods. And the roses. Then she'd send over one of the hands to swish the goats home—"Get home, you nasty goats! You don't belong over here!"

"This went on and on," said McKenna, the plumber. "Then one day she pulled up in her car, got out, knocked at our door. She said, 'I want to take care of you. I've damaged your bushes. I enjoy nature.' She wrote a check. 'You go to a nursery,' she said, 'and you replace all these things that I've ruined.'

"She was fair about everything. We didn't want it. We hardly expected it. I mean, the kind of person Mrs. Parker was..."

She bought her meat at a little market on Lorain Street. One chilly day in April she went in and ordered a nice plump half of cow. Then she said, "Hang it up in the freezer, I'll be back to pick it up." Months went by and the mold on it grew to over an inch in thickness. The butcher called her—urged her—finally begged her to come fetch it.

"No, let it hang a little longer," she insisted.

After awhile it was all the meat man could do just to walk into the cooler, but a few weeks later Adele came in to take a look at things. She dug into the mold with a small knife. She poked at the cow. . .

"Just right! Now cut it up into fourteen steaks!"

Then she said to the butcher, "You're invited—I'm having a little steak party!"

Later he admitted, "Believe it or not, those were the best steaks I ever had in my life. The woman knows meat! You'd never sell it to any American, but, my God, the woman knows meat!"

Earlier at the store he had started to carve the side of beef into fourteen steaks and Adele picked up a rusty knife and started giving him a hand.

"Aren't you going to wipe that off?" he asked.

"No, this is how we did out in the west—the old west," she said. It was enough of an explanation.

"When we moved in next door," said Jerry McKenna, "there was a small pony barn in the back, a small pigeon coop and a chicken coop. I casually mentioned to Mrs. Parker that I was going to tear down the pigeon house.

"Oh, don't tear it down!" she begged. "I'll have my boys come over there. We'll cut the fence and we'll push it through the fence and I have a spot *way out in back* and I'd love to put it there!"

"That's fine, Mrs. Parker. Rather than tear it down, I'd like to see you have it."

(After all, she had thirty-eight buildings there already. What was one more?)

"She sent over four of her finest hands. We got the little pigeon house up on rollers and she was directing everything like it was the Brooklyn Bridge or something. We shoved the pigeon coop through the fence. We hadn't pushed it two feet

through, when—"PUT THE FENCE BACK UP FOR MR.
MC KENNA—THAT'S FAR ENOUGH! I'VE CHANGED
MY MIND! LEAVE IT RIGHT THERE! I'M GOING TO
BUILD A LITTLE ZOO IN IT..."

"If I had known that—I was SICK of looking at it. I
wanted it OUT! You know? So there I am, *still* looking at
the same pigeon coop, except now it's just under my kitchen
window... I tell you—*anything* I had here that I wanted to
get rid of... like I took a bunch of fencing down. There's a
lot of fencing around here. It got on my nerves..."

"Oh, Mr. McKenna—what are you doing with the fencing?"

"Where do you want me to put it, Mrs. Parker?"

He put it in the wheelbarrow and wheeled it back there.

"Oh, the boys will take care of it."

They put it back on the pile and I think if you went back
there today you'd still see it on the pile. But she simply
could not reconcile an object being ruined, destroyed or discarded. All things had their place.

"I sat there every day," said Jerry McKenna, "looking with
dread at that chicken house of mine, and plotted to get rid of
it. It needed paint, lumber, hours of work. It *really* was in
bad shape. One day I came home and started taking the
boards off. I threw 'em in a pile and started burning 'em.
Out the door she flew—

"Mr. McKenna! Mr. McKenna! What are you doing?

"Oh, I'm going to tear my chicken house down!"

"Oh, no!"

"Mrs. Parker, you don't want it—it's full of TERMITES! I
seen the termites! They're walkin' toward your brand new
barn. If they ever hit that building, it will fall down..."

"Oh, don't let *that* happen! Burn it up—I'll send help!"

("I only wished I'd thought of that with the pigeon house").

Three weeks later, about six in the evening, a car came
racing in the driveway and a fellow flew into the house.
Then I saw Ramona, a boarder, jump in the truck and follow
him out again, and moments later they roared back in again
in a cloud of dust and wild commotion. The back of the truck
opened and they hauled out a mammoth deer. It had been

78

struck by a car in the valley and they had had to get it out of there before the police came.

They hauled the deer to Mrs. Parker's apple tree.

"Oh that's fine," she exclaimed. "That's elegant food!"

It had been lying on the side of the road for hours, for God's sake, and they hung it in the apple tree. A little colored fellow, maybe 65 or so, was standing there—Old Eddie. He says, "I know how to butcher." so Mrs. Parker says, "Okay, you butcher him."

The colored fella takes the knife and puts it into the chest of the deer, and Mrs. Parker yells, "It's going to be just like the old west, sure enough!" They drained the deer, hanging him in the apple tree, and she announced she was going to drain him to the very last drop.

"Years ago," she said, "this is how they did it and we're going to do it the same way now." She said, "I'm going to tan the hide, too!"

Eventually they commenced to remove the carcus and every fly in the valley came up to get in on it. Manley, the barnhand, then hoisted the whole deer over his shoulder. Mrs. Parker said, "What are you doin? Where you taking that deer to?"

He walked into the house with the corpse and blood's running down his back and all over the floor and the evening supper.

"I'm gonna wash him off," he said.

"No!" she roared. "Let him age—let the flies on there! A little blood never hurt nobody! Let the flies on there—that's what makes good meat!"

Two days later she knocked on her neighbor's door.

"Mr. McKenna, I have a beautiful piece of venison for you. . ."

Politely as he could, he declined. He wanted no part of it. He had seen the preliminaries.

"Our only real concern with the ranch," McKenna explained, "was the fast-driving cars up and down the driveway—because of our little boy. We hadn't lived here long when Mrs. Parker came to our door."

"Don't worry about those cars!" she said. "I'm going to

79

take care of *that!* I'm going to make a sign!"

"A few days later," said McKenna, "we saw her out by the mail box with a large easel and a can of brushes. By the time we got out there to thank her, the sign read, 'SLOW DOWN! CAUTION! TAKE IT EASY! BE CAREFUL OF HORSES, CATS, DUCKS, PIG, GOATS, DOGS, COW—

"Oh, Mr. McKenna!" she said, enthusiastically, "Did you say you have just *one* youngster? You do? Wonderful!"

She had just room enough to pencil in ". . . and child!"

"My boy was out there, a kid of maybe twelve or thirteen," said Karl Stats, the volunteer ranch helper, "and two girls came out, seventeen or eighteen, wanting horses. Mrs. Parker got 'em horses and my boy was their guide and he took them down trail, saying, 'Now do you want to go around this way or through the woods?'

"Oh, through the *woods!*"

"He took 'em and they got scratched up. That evening out comes the mother. And she is furious!

"You sent my girls down in the valley with a twelve-year-old kid?"

"Mrs. Parker said, 'Yes. What's wrong with that?'

"Why—a twelve-year-old boy taking two girls in the valley—on horses?"

"Mrs. Parker said, 'That boy is one of the most capable horsemen that I have ever known and your daughters could not have been in any better hands. Now,' she said, 'I know my responsibility—and I couldn't send your daughters or anybody's daughters down if they weren't properly protected. And anytime your daughters come out here to ride, if they can have *that* young fella, you'll never have to worry because if a horse acts up, he'll be right there to take care of them.'

"That mother," Stats said, "went home perfectly satisfied that Mrs. Parker had done the most proper thing for her daughters. Well, Adele had sold another bill of goods. True, my boy could ride. And I think if a horse took out, he'd try to catch it—but the fact remains that Parker sold this woman completely. I mean SHE COULD SELL! She had sold her on the idea that she had done everything absolutely right."

Listed simply as "trick riders" in the Parker's Ranch wild west show souvenier program, young ladies such as Marty Harmon of Fairview Park (above) joined the ranks of professional daredevils in coming within a hairbreadth of catastrophe two shows a day.

The coach (Mrs. Parker) and her kids polo team, 1949

CHAPTER 5

AND GLADLY TEACH

"We admired her. Indeed, we loved her, for she was still her own legend," smiled the breeder-trainer. "But she was not a teacher. Despite the stories and the sentiment, she was not even a horseman. But then again at Parker's Ranch, everything was and it wasn't. In the last twenty years horse shows have come a long way. They have evolved into specialized riding. You ride either a gaited horse or a western horse or a hunter horse. There are these classes!

"But Mrs. Parker would take the same horse into *any* class—just change her clothes and hop in there! You don't *do* that any more. You have one type all the way. Just like farming. You're a specialized farmer. You don't have a general farm any more. You have cattle or chickens. You have a lot of 'em and you have to keep track of 'em. Everything down pat all the way through.

"But Mrs. Parker would not accept that. Parker's was Parker's. It was not even open to the outside world half the time, and if it was, the outside world was wrong and Parker's was right. It was always that way."

"From May until late Autumn," the newspaper story read, "Sunday afternoons are times of activity at Parker's Ranch. After the races, the musical chairs, the mount-dismount exercises, and the wrestling on horseback, the real exhibition begins. By this time the Sunday motorists have ridden to the edge of the field. The cars are parked two and three deep. The last youngster rides off the side of the field as Mrs. Parker appears on Alexander MacDonald, reeling and plunging as he goes through his multiple paces—waltzing, marching, kneeling, rearing.

"Mrs. Parker sweeps her broad-brimmed sombrero from her head with a smile and bows low over the black maned, proudly curved neck of Alex, her braids hanging down on either side of her head.

"Mrs. Parker is happy.

"She has her public back again."

"Children are important," she once said. "I was out in California in 1926 doing some movies and a little portrait painting. I was riding down a street in Los Angeles when a little tot stepped off the curb and looked up at my mare, Daisy. She asked me what it was. It was then I decided to teach children.

"Didn't know what a horse was!" she said.

She built a small barn on a lot in South Pasadena. The children came down in the evenings to watch her work her horses. She got them together in her spare time and formed the Junior Rough Riders group. When they came to sign up, they could barely write. She made a deal. The worst offenders had to write the alphabet ten times and show improvement before they could get a horse ready, and sign their names legibly before they could ride.

The feed man came once a week for his bill. She would take out her purse and empty it on the tail gate of his truck.

"I let on I didn't know what arithmetic is," she said. "I would ask the kids to help me figure what to pay the feed man. Then they went to school and asked their teachers to teach them so they could teach me. I talked to some of the parents and we arranged it so that their youngsters could sneak out of the house at night and come down and teach me arithmetic by candle light. It was very secret, you know. They worked hard to educate me," she grinned.

Her barn was at the foot of a hill, bordered by the gardens of a large estate. It was owned by a man, well along in years, and irascible. He had a particular aversion to children. He went to see the district attorney and registered a complaint. Then he started circulating a petition to evict the Parker tribe on grounds that they were in a registered neighborhood. The D.A. came to look things over.

"I was checking over the day's lessons when he came," Mrs. Parker said. "He asked me what I was doing. I told him I was organizing some arithmetic. He asked me if I was a teacher and I told him about our system. He laughed. 'Come over to my office,' he said, 'and I'll give you a petition, too.'

"I got the petition and my bunch took it around. It came

84

back with two hundred signatures and more remarks than you can think of."

The Junior Rough Riders planned a show, but there were difficulties finding a place to seat an audience. Mrs. Parker thought the hillside would be ideal. She went up to the big house a few times to call.

"I got him to come down and look around," she said. "He told me he had disowned his daughter when she was married. He had some grandchildren but never had seen them."

The neighborhood turned out for the Junior Rough Riders show. They sat on the side of the hill and were served soft drinks and candy. The man up at the big house picked up the bill.

In 1931, the idea of a woman instructor of horsemanship was still suspect. Men were hesitant about putting themselves or their children up on a horse and relying on a woman to get them out of trouble. Mrs. Parker never tried forcing minds that were made up. She just kept succeeding.

To the best of my memory, no one was killed or maimed at Parker's Ranch. Dozens came close.

"I kept holding on to that same hunk of Blondie's mane as I took the jumps," Helen Shaunessey recalls. "We were tying down the fine points of proper body position without holding on, but I was so scared I cheated. In moments, that hunk of Blondie's mane weakened and pulled out and I went under his front legs and chopped up one leg—chopped it and chewed it.

"Mrs. Parker was right there and much to Eugenia's consternation she got out the good wool horse bandage which was a crying shame. You don't wrap people with good horse bandage! She also took the good beef which Eugenia had ready for supper. Ground beef and ice crushed together in an oozy blend. She packed my leg in the stuff and wrapped it in the red horse bandage.

"When I reached home I simply said, 'Mom, I kind of hurt my leg.'

"She looked at this red bandage.

"I said, 'I fell under a horse.'

"She had a gargantuan fear of horses, anyway, and had

terrible thoughts of what might have happened, having seen me pitched over the ears once, and unwrapping this thing she looked upon the soggy, raw meat which had turned to slush. Without uttering so much as a word or a sound, she fainted dead away on the living room floor."

"Traveler," Dorothy Carmichael explained, "was a psychotic horse—he really was. Sometimes he could be very normal and nice. But he'd go after you in the stall and he'd go after you on the ground—also when you were astride him. Yet I pestered her to let me ride him. All the horses get hot in the spring. They're hard to ride. Even most gentle horses kick up. I had ridden some of her prestige horses already. But this one was even higher on the hierarchy.

"Going down hill was a place where you stopped to rest the horses. When you stopped HIM there, he'd rear straight up, sometimes spring over backwards. I mean I've seen him fall down the valley hill—that's how nuts he was.

"Mrs. Parker always said a *good* horse would protect itself.

"This one didn't.

"She kept saying the horse is too tough.

" 'Wait a little bit.'

"The third time I asked, she looked me very straight. It was mucky and cold, though it was springtime. Then she asked, 'Are you sure you can do it?'

"Yes."

"All right."

"I had had this on my mind for a whole year. She said okay and told someone to saddle him up. She said, 'I suggest you don't—but if you must. . .'

"I had to wait two hours. I think she was giving me time to change my mind. She had the horse brought out. I got on Trav on the mounting block right in front of the second barn. I don't remember whether I was led to the ring or whether I walked. Oh, I felt great—like a million dollars. Here I was on this horse and it was beautiful. I got into the ring and closed the gate.

"Suddenly the horse went up all the way around and he was feeling like dynamite and I was scared. Still I was going to show Mrs. Parker that I really could ride him. Then he exploded into ten thousand pieces. He reared up again, bucked, flashed around, way up high—I got dumped in the mud. The horse took off, went for the fence—but she was there. She got him. The horse was still acting crazy as hell. I was embarressed, full of mud, wet and cold.

"I got on my bike," regrets Dorothy Carmichael, "and went home down Gessner Road, weeping the whole way, thinking to myself, 'Goddam it, some day I'm going to ride that horse!'"

But it took her a year to do it again.

"What attracted people to Mrs. Parker?" the local banker observed. "Her attitude! I don't care whether people rode or not, her *attitude* was the thing that set everybody up. She always had a remark for this little horse and that little horse. They went for her, too. And if a kid wasn't happy on a horse, she took him right down because that was inconsistent to her as to the way things should be."

To teach what a horse would do, she became a horse. She'd put a lead between her teeth and you walked behind her. But you had to be careful. She was quick with her feet. She kicked and bit. She wore those boots with the high heels and they hurt.

"Whether the rider is on the ground, on her head, or on her backside," said instructor Patty Harding, "the rein should be in her left hand. If she falls off on the right side, it should be in her right hand. Adele demonstrated to me with Winchester how it should be done and then she had me do it several times to make sure that I knew what she meant——and that I could teach it—and I have taught it ever since the way she said.

"There are three methods for "flying dismount" (I have taught two) where you get off like Douglas Fairbanks Jr.—throw your leg over and jump off, or in case of trouble and the horse is moving very fast—you kick your feet out of the stirrups, lie forward on him with your arms around his neck, then use your arms to hold you back. You throw your legs over and at just the right beat of the trot or canter, you let go and push free of the animal.

"She taught how to do that with the rein, too. And if you

make sure you don't let go, even though he's cantering very fast, your movement off of him will stop him and if it doesn't stop him, your grip and dragging that rein will stop him. He won't drag you far.

"I have seen it done," said Patty Harding, "and it works. My daughter ended up in the hospital with stitches in her head and blood all the way down her back, but she said, 'Mom, I hung on.' The animal dragged her through the gravel but she wouldn't let go. Finally she had to let go because he broke into a canter and she saw the barn coming up fast and it had a concrete floor.

"She said it hurt so bad she had to let go. She started to pass out. But it does work. You can stay with your horse to a point."

"She would repeatedly remind people," recalls instructor Frances Bibbs, "the horse always comes first if it is uncomfortable, hurt, if it's wet and dirty, if it's tired and sweaty. It comes first and then you take care of yourself. Because'—and years ago I would ask her why and she would answer, 'Frances, that horse is there because you want him there. He isn't there because he wants to be. If he had his own way he'd be out running free with nobody on his back, doing as he pleases. Therefore, if he's uncomfortable, tired, hungry, he comes first. Then you

"One day the message came she wanted to see me—to name the day or just go over. 'She wants to see you about something very important.' So I went over three times for the entire day. Each time I came home depressed because it just seemed she was trying to cram everything she had learned and known in her lifetime into those few days. She taught me these things and said, 'These are the ways I wish you to teach.' "

Youngsters frequently inquired what it would take to be as great a rider as their Mrs. Parker.

"One has only so many hours to live," Frances Bibbs would explain, "and if those hours are spent doing one thing, you learn so much faster, you have so many more experiences, and you learn much better about that thing. Now if you only go horseback riding and you pay somebody six dollars for private lessons once a week, by the time you're the age she was when she died, you don't know much about a horse. You have to *be* with them hour after hour after hour. So when I get to be the age she was, will I be as good a rider? No—there were too many years spent away from horses.

"And so you lose—you lose your ability to handle them. You lose your own balance. It takes so long to get it back. Her experiences were so many and so packed tight—and just constant horses, horses, horses—perhaps two hundred or three hundred at a time! Well, who has that opportunity?

"Nobody. . ."

Never that I know of did Adele Parker consciously cheat anybody. Never, according to her own values. But eventually things would occur which forced her to lower her standards just a pinch. Lo and behold, people still came. Later, due to other problems, she lowered her standards a little more. They still came. And she lowered her standards lower still, and the people still came. And then she got older and would stay in the house and have the kids take care of things—and they still came. . . to the point that in later years, she wasn't entering in at all. The kids did it all. They did everything.

Then the people started to stay away.

With affection, rider Ellen Burgess recalls the black stallion, Alex MacDonald.

"When I started riding him," Ellen grinned, "I was too dumb to realize you shouldn't ride stallions in company with mares. And Parker never told me anything. She just gave me a lead bat and said, 'If he makes any trouble, beat him over the nose with it.' I rode him bareback in company for years and never knew I was risking anything, and then, of course, some woman—I don't know where she was from—wanted so much to ride Alex because he was so beautiful.

"Mrs. Parker kept putting her off, putting her off. Finally she said, 'If you ride him, you do it at your own risk. I cannot be responsible.'

'The woman got down trail. Alex turned around and bit off her toe right through her boot.

"She did not ask again."

Mrs. Parker felt strongly that there was one sure cure for all ailments in the world and that cure was horseback riding. You had the weight off your feet. You had proper massage. It took care of vericose veins, kidney ailments, malfunctioning of the digestive track. Of course you could get other problems *from* horseback riding such as bad knees (which most of us have) but when that happened, you merely sent for a bone setter.

Generations of Parker riders shared one thing in common—the order to hang onto a horse's neck. "*That* is your best friend on a horse!" she insisted. "If anything goes wrong, hang onto his neck because a horse's body is going to follow its head! Just drop your hands to his neck. In jumping, *always* do so. Wherever he whips, you'll follow right along."

Other teachers frown on that.

"Grab leather!" they say. "Take hold of the saddlehorn! Anything leather!" Still others say, "Oh, you mustn't do those things! You must put your hands high in the air—even if the horse whips out from under you!"

Parker saw that as ridiculous. "Save your neck!" she'd say. "You can learn to be pretty *later*."

Children had seen the TV and the movies of the old west. But here was the real thing. This wasn't *play* cowboy. They *were* cowboys. And Mrs. Parker had each little youngster teach another youngster. As fast as some little imp was on anything at all, no matter how simple it was—"Now you go over and show that little boy how to do this!"

She always sat on the picnic table right in front of the riding ring. You couldn't make a wrong move. She'd catch it. She always sat there. The instructors would be in the ring, she sat on the table. She'd just holler her head off if something went amiss. One time my horse rolled and scared me. I wouldn't get on the horse again so she got me on an old plug and sent me out. She said, "You're not going to stay off a horse!" She made you feel rotten if you wouldn't do a thing she commanded. You did it or were humiliated.

She didn't believe in your riding a horse, either, if you couldn't bridle it, curry it, clean it. You didn't come out there just to ride—this was a thing she made very plain. You came out there to be *taught* riding.

And she showed you in comparison to your own body how you would look if you looked like a horse. She compared everything to *you*. Learning the parts of a horse, she would say, "Now if you bent over, where would your hip bone be? Where would it be on a horse? And she made the horse you. "If you want to go forward, you *lean* forward. If you want to stay still, you simply stand there. You can't lean forward and not fall over. You can't lean forward on a horse and expect him to stand stock still!"

Like most everybody, Adelaide Briggs, a young woman of twenty, was frightened of her.

"I would avoid one of her tantrums at any cost," she confessed. "But this one day my horse was sopped with perspiration. He was very, very hot and we both were tired. There was a jumping course set up in the front. Mrs. Parker said, 'Okay, now go and jump your horse.' That's when I had to quit, so I said, 'No, I'm sorry, Mrs. Parker, because I'm not up to it at this point.' The horse was so hot he would have killed me. I'm not kidding. The horse would have taken off with me and killed me if he could.

"Mrs. Parker looked at me with a disbelieving stare—then said, 'Well. What's for supper?' "

The Hungarian lady fresh from Europe was interested in dressage. She had a big Palomino horse, a big jumper.

"I had apparently done well with my horse, Judge," she reported, "a very high-spirited animal, but he was crazy and I went to Parker's Ranch in an effort to have him calmed down. The first lesson fell on a scorching hot afternoon. I really was interested in having the horse sedated by walking and trotting. But rather she saw that he had a lot of action and she said, 'Okay, change canter, change leads one-two, one-two! Turn on the four! Shoulder in, shoulder out!' And of course my animal wasn't at all ready for this.

"I mean he didn't even know what I was doing. In fact I was getting him so loused up at this point, he just refused to go forward. He just stood still. Then every time I asked him to go forward, he'd start running backward and begin kicking. Mrs. Parker of course loved this. She had me do all these silly things to correct him and get him to high-step.

"What I'm trying to say is she got me a little disappointed by that time. . ."

Attorney for Mrs. Parker's defense in all matters of horsemanship and humanity could well have been Frieda Geiger, a brisk and worshipful farm woman from Lorain County.

"Whatever else she was or wasn't," howled Frieda, "she was a *magnificent teacher!* She taught ya how to ride and if you fell off, she didn't have much mercy on ya—boom! Get up and ride 'em! Other teachers might baby ya—feel ya all over to see if you had broken bones. . . *She* plopped you right back on, slapped the horse's behind and watched you take off! One thing Mrs. Parker was a bug on—you didn't learn out of no books!"

At the ranch Mrs. Parker kept A, B and C horses. She said she could tell by the manner a person first approached a horse, how she patted him, whether she understood him, whether she was afraid or whether she loved. I never got the friskiest. I got a halfway horse—a "B" horse.

Abuse an animal—hers or any other's—and you signed your own death warrant with Adele Parker. We had gone over to the fairgrounds one Saturday to officiate at the horse show. There she met Louise, her pupil, who brought a little rag-tail pony, a rugged little fellow. But Louise had three or four kids on that pony the whole time we were there—racing up and down, up and down. Mrs. Parker grumbled and groaned and grunted and complained the whole time. Before we left, she simply went over and said, "You don't deserve this animal." She simply took it home, leaving the children standing there. She called the mother, explaining what she had done and why. The mother said, "Thank you very much."

At Parker's, when you started to jump, you got up a foot or two and you did it without the reins and without the stirrups so that your balance was perfected. Most kids had visions of going three bars the first day, but she taught that you go step by step and before you go charging off to do the glorious thing, you go back and do the steady necessary preliminaries. When you're ready, you won't be in trouble.

These were very valuable lessons. We thought we were learning to ride—and all the while we were learning life.

Entirely unpredictable, her sham tantrums were a part of her attraction, an ingredient of her mischief.

"I started to ride with a western saddle," laughed Phylis Krueger, the Lakewood, Ohio, fourth-grade teacher, "Because that's what I thought you were supposed to do. For one thing, you have that thing to hang on to in front. I went out there one time and Mrs. Parker was back on the mounting block.

"Well, how are you, my dear?"

"I'd like to ride."

"What horse, my sweet?"

"I'd like to have Sis."

"What kind of saddle do you wish?"

"Oh, western—"

"WELL ANYBODY WHO CAN'T SADDLE HER OWN HORSE HAS NO RIGHT TO RIDE WESTERN! SHOULDN'T RIDE IF YOU CAN'T GET YOUR OWN HORSE READY! *GADS*—WESTERN SADDLE!"

She taught children just a lot about being nice people. You'd ride downtrail with her and there'd be a whole string of kids. She'd say, "I bet the kids in the hospital would like to trade places with us for a little while." Another time she'd get ready to take you home and she'd say, "Are you in a hurry? I got a couple of stops to make." She'd fill up a few baskets with things from the little garden in back and drop them off for people.

Without making sermons about things, she was inspiring. She subtly taught caring for people and appreciating your blessings—of *giving a damn.*

In almost all cases within the confines of my memory, she did not put on airs. She never strived to be something she wasn't. You liked her or you didn't. She helped a generation grow up better. Riding, to her, wasn't simply a matter of sitting on a horse and looking pretty. It was also plopping your hands in manure.

93

"Know the basics of life," she insisted. "No matter the emergency or contingency, you will survive in spite of great fear."

"I remember," the psychologist said, "the day they brought Judy home. "Out like a light. Dangling. I don't know who brought her. A young man. She was unconscious, having been thrown. She had ridden Phantom and I don't know just what she had done. But I know Judy. She was apt to be doing precisely what she shouldn't.

"She let Phantom get the bit between his teeth and she had been told what to do in that event. But she decided if she leaned forward she could loosen it, and tried to, just as Phantom went over a log. He threw her and she was out for three days. They brought her home and I put her to bed. The doctor said, 'Leave her there. Don't move her!'

"When she came to, she remembered nothing. At the end of a week, I checked with the doctor and said I'd like to take her back and get her on a horse. 'I don't care if she ever rides again,' I insisted, 'I don't want her afraid of anything!' I took her back out there and put her on Lucky Strike.

"Adele was calm. Lucky Strike had brought Judy up from the valley. Consequently it would be fair for Lucky Strike to take her back down (this was Adele).

"Judy was little. She cried and begged not to be made to get on the horse. Mrs. Parker just got on *her* horse and said they were going. I stood there and said, 'You've got to. I know you're afraid but you've got to go.'

"They went and from where I stood I could see Mrs. Parker pointing out an early blooming jonquil on the rim of her valley world."

"If a child was injured," explained the vet, "she would not say, 'Oh, I'm so worried about you, Charley.' She could only express her concern with a scold and a reprimand. Perhaps in her own family you just didn't express compassion. You simply *didn't express it*. So instead of verbal entreaties, she lifts the unconscious rider in her arms and says, 'If I told you once, I've told you a thousand times, NEVER TAKE A JUMP LIKE THAT!'

"This was *her* compassion, her outward indication of con-

94

cern. She couldn't show it any other way. And in such sternness, there was great warmth."

She believed completely that *enjoyment* was the key to good riding—that you have a marvelous time with your horse. Some teach a military method. That everything should be *this* way! *this* way! *this* way! With Mrs. Parker, no matter *how* you looked or how your horse looked, YOU MUST BE ENJOYING IT—and the horse must be enjoying *you* as a rider.

If the two of you aren't seeing eye to eye and aren't having fun, no matter *how good you look,* you better get off. Put him in the barn. If you're fighting him and he's fighting you in order to make him look good, yes, he's better off in the barn—*you're* better off shopping in downtown Cleveland.

"Weak people were in trouble with Mrs. Parker," smiled ranch secretary Mary Rankin. "I'm talking about a particular kind of weakness—not shyness. She understood shyness. The other kind of weakness—the person who lies on the ground and says, 'Well, I give up'—she wouldn't tolerate. As long as people were in there fighting and trying to do something, she could respect them. And so you got along with her. The kind of weakness I'm talking about is the namby-pamby weakness where there is no inner-strength and no potential for any. This is the thing. A person who couldn't be challenged—couldn't make it with her."

"I was riding in the valley," recalled a young woman, "just to get used to a horse, and she began correcting the way I held the reins. Then she caught herself and said, 'No, you're riding for pleasure! That's all right.' But then all the way through the ride, she kept saying, 'That's almost it, just put your thumbs here, or do this!' By the time we got halfway down Parker's Hill, she decided she didn't want me riding the horse I was on. I was to ride hers. We switched. She scared me to death. I lived in terror of making a mistake. I was eight. She terrorized me. I loved her madly.

"Later, I was eighteen and in college the time my little sister attended Parker's. I went over one day with Sis just to see how things had changed. Parker recognized me immediately. Well, I was eighteen, a big girl. Not the little girl who took lessons anymore. I was truly happy to see her. But in her way, which was rather brusk, she merely said, 'Hello, I'm happy to see you. Some of these kids are having trouble mounting. Get out there and show them what to do!'

"I was right back to eight years old again. I was up and on the horse. There I was riding behind Peg in the saddle in good wool slacks which I then had to throw out—while she yelled, 'Show her *this,* show her *that!* HEY! You haven't forgotten!'

"And I mean—she said it and I did it."

She never complimented you very much. Still, she was this mystical figure in a child's eyes—all powerful and the one person to whom you always went with a problem. . . Maybe once, maybe twice a year she would see you out in the ring riding and would call you aside afterwards and tell you you had really done well.

This you would hold on to. You might get screamed at by Eugenia, Mary or Mrs. Parker for the next four months, but no matter; there was that one time.

It would sustain you.

Her physical condition was incredible. I saw her take a fall off a horse while showing us something and she hit so hard you could feel it. She lay there a minute. Then she got up and walked back over. Just this once I asked, "Are you all right?"

Parker said, "It's the funniest thing—I've had a charley horse for a week. I can't seem to work it out." It's all she ever said about it. Of course, we were expected to respond similarly to anything that happened to us.

"Oh, you have a headache?" she asked as you went off a jump on your head.

"It'll be fine."

A woman like her could have glorified rebellion and won a clear following. In no way did she do so. Oddly enough, she sanctified respect.

"She simply asked me to hold four or five horses," explained the mother of a student, "none of whom liked each other and had to be kept separate. It never occurred to her that I didn't like horses. I never would have told her and she wouldn't have believed it. She wouldn't believe that my feelings for my children would be so strong that I wouldn't sit there and hold somebody's goddam horses. I *had* to like horses. Naturally I did. Why else would I be there? So I sat and held horses.

"But I watched my daughter Judy riding and I think she had not been riding more than a month when Mrs. Parker put her on Traveler, which was unheard of. She let her jump him. Judy was new, bull-headed, definitely 'I can do it myself!' So Traveler took the jump and Judy took it ahead of him. She went too far forward and came down *whack!*

"My impulse as a mother—holding five goddam horses——was 'Ah-h-h-h-h-h!' Mrs. Parker was sitting beside me on the fence and she jumped, hitting the ground the same instant Judy did, but she never took one step forward. She waited to see if she got up and if she got up, what she would do. Judy got up, went after Traveler and caught him. Mrs. Parker came back on the fence.

"She never said a word. I don't think she even noticed me. This was her world and not my world. I really didn't know anything about it. When I trusted my child to her, I trusted her completely. I knew that if she were needed, she would go, and if she didn't go, it was because she wasn't needed."

Mrs. Parker's domestic life would have made a delightful stage play.

"I watched Mrs. Parker shop," smiled the dentist, "and these bananas were all priced out at Rinis at so much a bunch—20¢ for this bunch, 40¢ for that. She said, "I don't like it when they're all priced like that! I just want *this banana* from this bunch"—it was a 35¢ bunch. So she simply pulled it off, but instead of choosing a second banana from the same bunch, she went clipping through and found another banana from another bunch and put just the two bananas on the scale."

Indeed, I remember how angry and mortified she was the day she walked into a bank and was told she had to have collateral for a loan. Her WORD was her bond! It isn't that kind of world. Adele von Ohl Parker thought it *should* be.

Once, Russ and Curly Janus were sitting out at the picnic

table with Mrs. Parker who was explaining that her mother had been the incentive to them all. She had told Adele always to be a lady. "Always be a lady—whether you ride horses or what—always be a lady!" At just that moment a truck came down Mastick Road spraying for bugs. She started screaming though we were far from the road. She shrieked, "Stop that! Stop that! We got horses here!" She leaped from the table, got in her car and chased the truck far down the road.

"What did she say?" asked Russ.

"Be a lady," Curly said.

She was a fount of pharmaceutical expertise.

She vigorously prescribed vinegar for scratches, mud for soreness in the legs. She built a "health bath" out at the side for the horses to stand in. She never could get them in it. They elected no part of it. But her *ideas* were good, and she had a sackful of those. She took sweet cream and just smeared it all over herself. She rubbed it over her face, then threw it at the cat, and she had a paper ear trumpet made of rolled newspaper.

She lit one end and as it burned, the ink vapor bellowed into her ears, curing the earache. She brewed up black leaf tea which was just like the white of an egg, all in one string. She would make this order up and it would look like the spawn of fish or frogs. And she peddled pills made of alfalfa and they were supposed to make you live forever.

"My son Bobby came down with a cold," recalled the plumber's wife, Jean McKenna, "and though it was bitter cold outside I bundled him up good and took him in the buggy. Mrs. Parker said, 'Jean, if you want to get rid of Bobby's cold, you wheel this buggy into the barn and let Bobby smell the horse manure.' She assured me it was the very best thing for a cold. I wheeled him by the door just to satisfy her."

Everybody who came there she'd take aside and tell how unhealthy most foods were. She was equally sure that the reason so many persons were having emotional troubles was because they didn't go barefoot as they were meant to. When men went into the fields in bare feet behind the plow, she reasoned, they picked up the electricity from the ground and the vitality of the earth.

The Elyria, Ohio mother of five regretted disappointing Mrs. Parker that September in the 1960's.

"My husband had been ill with an ulcer," she explained. "Naturally with that discomfort, his stomach was not strong. Mrs. Parker was determined he would take goats milk for it. In his sensitive condition, it was all he had to hear, but she was persistent. She assured me she could have fresh goats milk over here fifteen minutes after she flushed it from the udders."

A few comers and goers felt the one good thing about those goats was the stickers people put on your car that nobody could get off. When the goats were there, you never had trouble. They ate them off.

The small porch was decrepit and there was always some animal incarcerated on it until it got over its temporary trouble. The house itself I loved if only for its surprises. I was sitting in that bleached-walled kitchen one afternoon at sunset and, by God, I saw this thing waddling out from behind the stove. I looked at it and I looked at Mrs. Parker and I said, "What is it?"

She said, "That's a dog."

"That's a dog?"

"It's a dog."

"What kind?"

"She's a Pomeranian."

I said, "It looks like a porcupine!" and it did.

She was hurt because I did not know it was a dog.

She never cared about the number of animals in the house. Animals were the same as people. If they wanted to come into the house, let them come into the house. Animal droppings never bothered her. Occasionally, she'd call one of the barnhands to wash the dishes. This made the women so terribly ill they would re-wash everything a second and often a third time. Most food was kept in the refrigerator where there was rarely room for a cat to lie sideways, though a few had tried.

"When they start tearing the house down," people would

say, "there may be a million things you'll find in the walls. Not money—things she may not have wanted anyone to know she had—upstairs—in the attic. . ." Fact of the matter was that the floors were one board thick, so that with no trouble at all, one could stand in the cellar and peer up through them to the attic; or from the attic to the cellar. Still, rumors persisted that all kinds of treasures and mysteries lay stashed in those rafters. It was a physical impossibility.

In the front room you couldn't *find* the telephone. You had to DIG for the telephone. . . under the saddles, blankets and clothes. . . Once in awhile a cook would walk up the driveway. One of them took on the basement, ridding the walls of the grease the hands had splattered around. Once in awhile Mrs. Parker would storm down there with a bucket of suds and swash around along side him.

The house was a hodge-podge jungle of everything there could be. "I was out a few years ago," laughed a neighbor. "Mrs. Parker was holding a chicken in her lap—explaining the reason it hadn't developed just exactly as God intended was that it had grown up in the house over the winter. In the bathtub, I believe. . ."

For many years there was no running water in the house. There was a pump in the sink. As time went on, the water lines were put in which repeatedly froze, or for other reasons had to be repaired. One of the more serious adjustments Mrs. Parker faced was the Health Department's order to put in flush toilets in spite of the more reliable holes in the ground.

Each year the Christmas tree stayed out on the porch until it literally dried out and disintegrated into crumbs and needles which bodies, coming and going incessantly, tracked in and out. Barely a skeleton remained come May when someone mercifully dragged the remains out back and laid them to rest.

In one room they had the sick rabbit. They called a doctor and he came. The rabbit quickly ran under the davenport and they said, "Doctor, please wait, just wait—your patient will be out in a moment." The MD is sitting there waiting and the rabbit runs across to a chair and they said, "There's

100

your patient." The doctor looked—and it struck him so funny that he called another doctor on the telephone. "I can't figure out what the sam hill's wrong!" he said. "Please come over right away—*hurry!*" Both doctors spent the whole evening chasing after the ailing bunny which flitted from sofa to chair to icebox.

"She invited me to see some paintings," laughed a neighbor, "but the cat had a rat it had just caught and was sitting eating it in the pantry, and I just thought, 'Oh, my God! I don't *know,* now!' I figured she was letting things go down hill a bit. Of course the cat was happy. . ."

Her young riders recall strips of fly paper all over the house but mostly in the kitchen. The old *bench* symbolized the kitchen—that and the large pail and the grate. How many hundreds of time we came in after a hard ride, hiked our buttocks up to that grate and toasted them there. Few recall two pieces of furniture in the house that matched, or more than three pans in the place, one beat-up old coffee pot and a mason jar full of spoons. A vivid memory was raising the foal in the dining room. The mother died and Parker dragged the baby horse in and sprinkled straw over everything.

During the summer in the good weather, the Parker dogs might put themselves out to go gr-r-r-r at the cat, and the Parker cat might pause to whack the Parker rabbit (though creatures *rarely* diddled with the rabbit). Come winter, though, and the cold, they all could be found sprawled on a saddle blanket before the fireplace, side by side—cat, dog, rabbit, cat duck, dog, rabbit, dog, Mrs. Parker. . .

"I'd invite her here for dinner," an old friend smiled. "She appreciated it. I'd try to set a nice table with the best silver and the good china. She yearned to play the Grande Dame and would say, 'I just *love* to come here!' We'd eat by candlelight and it would be calm and peaceful—then she'd go promptly to the couch, fall asleep and snore."

The mother of little girls made a face and said, "At times she would think me odd. Just too fussy and prissy. But I couldn't eat at Parker's Ranch, that's all! Nor would my husband ever touch a thing in that house. I simply don't appreciate steaks where animals' asses have rubbed about. Parker boarders were endowed with a special tolerance for it—a certain stomach."

It was simply a matter of acclimation.

The food was never put away. It was on the table or on the counter. It was always there. Anyone who was hungry could have it. Bowls and bowls of spaghetti. Steaks that she obtained probably were the cheapest grade. I mean you paid so much for the overnight ride, food included. I never tasted anything so good in my life. In the morning, pancakes and hot chocolate, tea and clinkers (burnt toast). And apples off the apple tree.

She would take a cigarette now and then and take a puff. Not often. And at times she'd look at me and say, "You know, dear, you're the only one I know who smokes a cigarette correctly."

I never knew what to make of that.

Students still talk of her stopping and tying the horses, then pulling out one of her revolting looking concoctions. We'd be terribly hungry. She'd pull it out, throw it on a plate and say, "I don't suppose anybody wants any of these ugly looking things?" We'd sit there drooling, watching her devour her pancake-jelly-egg-and-bacon sandwich.

Often, on a Saturday or Sunday, there wouldn't be a drop of food in the house for the family. Oh, the men got fed. The horses got fed. All of the sudden—this magic. Someone would come in with a big ham. Thanksgiving. Christmas. Easter. It didn't have to be a holiday. Someone would come in with a turkey. One or two. A cake. A pie.

She'd just say, "Well. . . everybody eat!"

A cook I know said, "You're supposed to *bake* chicken pot pie. She *boiled* hers. She kept repeating, "Oh, God, that's good!" You could go down in her basement and Mrs. Parker would take something—an egg, say, and break it in a cup, stir it and eat it. She cleaned the cat with sour milk. Mrs. P. had a habit of coming into the house and commencing to clean the dog, picking all the dirt off of it, letting it drop. Then she made mincemeat for supper.

"Yes, but you get a gang of kids in there," defended the

blacksmith Walter Page, "you get a gang of horses in there. You got guys who should be workin' but they're not—they're out on a toot. The water's froze. Eugenia's tearin' her hair out. *Mary's* tearin' *her* hair out 'cause 'where are the goldang books that were right on this table?'

" 'Mrs. Price, you want to give me your money? All right, dear, you owe for three lessons? Certainly. Yes, dear, I'll write it down—as soon as I can find my goldang books.'

"Can you imagine the harassment there? You get the picture? I mean it's amazing *any* of 'em stood it. It's amazing Mrs. Parker had the courage to take that all them years. I mean the woman was *used*... I couldn't have tolerated it! I don't know *anyone* who could have tolerated it!"

Mrs. Parker had people who just drifted in and were taken care of. Like Harriet, the Hungarian nut with the goats. Parker knew Harriet's family way back. But she was Crazy Harriet. In her forties. She adored goats. Was slovenly. Wore rouge. And filthy—filthy like you've never seen. In the cellar were dirty old men and urine and food. It had nothing to do with the people upstairs. Those dirty old men who shoveled out the stalls. Some of them were strange.

Many were bums Adele had picked up and fed a meal to. They'd be there for a hundred years or a minute. Then there were the bunkhouse people, and others camping out in the trailers. There was a hierarchy there and each fit into his own pigeonhole. There was no transgressing. They automatically fell into it—like water seeking its own level. And the kids and everyone out there knew exactly where each of these dirty old people or whatever—fit.

It was the same with the children and the adult riders who came there, too. We'd sign up for horses—Carrie Jo or Allah or Happy Jack—if you rode these horses, you were on top of the heap—the rest of the campers realized with much envy that you had made it.

Anybody was allowed in. Any time. You were welcome, but you never went upstairs. I went there for five or six years and I never went upstairs. I don't know anybody who ever went upstairs. Once we had looked for days for sister Winnona's false teeth—literally turned the place upside

103

down. Then one of those fifteen Pomeranian pups came flying out from someplace carrying the teeth in its jowls. Winnona just said, "Thank you," and picked them up and put them in her mouth.

Mrs. Parker always said, "When you come to Parker's Ranch, bring your rubbers and put 'em on when you come *into* the house." Half of their dogs had no teeth. Nona would mix up mush and hold it in her hand. Boy, they had a mess of 'em there. None were housebroken. It was one of those things.

"I had locked myself out of the house," explained Jean McKenna, the plumber's wife next door. "My husband was working in the area and I had to call him to come open the door. I ran, barefooted, into Mrs. Parker's and caught all those rabbit marbles between my toes. I found the phone, finally, but it was *so dark* in there. There was so much dust from people coming in and out with their horses and not wiping their feet.

"It was hard to see well enough to dial but I finally managed and sat kicking these things off my toes. Running through the hall I could feel every one of them hitting and squashing. Mrs. Parker stood right there watching me and said not a word."

A young woman recalled the day Mrs. Parker found a check for $150 that was fifteen years old. "I lived on the first floor," she remembered. "We referred to the stairway as the 'wooden hill.' Jean and Mrs. Parker lived up on third. I never in my life was upstairs in that house."

Shopping was forever a mystery, a guess-what game. Mary seldom left til just before supper. Then Mrs. Parker also would come home with things. She refused to buy soap in large boxes. "A small box of Tide, please." Nor would they give thought to sales or bushel baskets of potatoes. "Five pounds, please..." That's how they bought. "Two cans of soup..."

At night when we'd go to the outhouse, old Jack, the chef on the Cream of Wheat box, would be wandering about. He wore a white kitchen rig and swung a cleaver. No one knew where he'd be going, what he'd be doing. Where did he come from? Who knows? They all drifted in and drifted out. He was just there.

All will recall sister Nona filling the upstairs tub to exercise the goldfish, then forgetting about it, and everything running over—water and thin little fish tinkling through the ceiling. Nor was it uncommon for the ice man to open the icebox on the back porch and have five cats jump out and five more jump in in the time it took to lower his ice. Then, "Shoo, shoo, shoo!" and close the lid.

She had rabbits in the cupboards in the pantry. She had a rabbit under the kitchen table. She had her Pomeranian dogs which urinated freely on the grate in the kitchen. She had a pony named Danny Boy who conveniently each morning succumbed to violent chill and had to be brought in and served liquor. She had a St. Bernard from time to time, and a Sicilian donkey.

Upstairs (for those who gained access) was a shambles. If you couldn't find it elsewhere, look in Nona's room. Nona was at the age where, if she saw a thing sitting around, she'd pick it up and take it to her room. She had a bale of hay under her bed in case they ran out.

Mrs. Parker had a quality that made you respect the lady *in* her, Winnona von Ohl *was* a lady. They were at odds continually. Yet so close. Nona wasn't the boisterous type. She wasn't like Parker—"HOW ARE YOU! Oh, I'm so glad to see you!" All that crap. Nona would say, "Hello, there," and that was it.

She perhaps had been a beautiful person in younger days but rarely dressed so that any beauty could show through. She would lose patience more quickly than Parker. I think she didn't like so goddam many kids fooling around.

Winnona had graying, naturally curly hair and a big nose and nice eyes and she was sweet and quiet. An excellent horse woman. She was sort of an unsung star about the place, I think. Did much to keep it going, God knows. But she was neither pretty nor handsome, as Mrs. Parker was. A much subdued, colorless human being. If you went to her for something, she was sweet and darling and had no magnetism.

105

"Winnona von Ohl?" asked the psychologist friend of the Parkers, "she referred to herself as Amelia in my presence. Perhaps it had been her stage name. Perhaps it was some sort of pretend thing. Who knows? Amelia admired Adele but was afraid of her. In my twenties, I was a corner mouse and she was a corner mouse. We'd talk while everybody else did what everybody else did. She talked about her sister and what they did as girls. Her happiest time, she told me, was when they toured the South and went to these beautiful homes. She talked of crystal chandeliers, lovely wine services, real gentlemen and real ladies.

"She saw it as something she could never have, would never really know. It saddened her, this fleeting, beautiful glimpse. She was like a child with her nose pressed against the candy store window.

"She was shorter than Adele. Not plump, but heavier. Adele was stocky and hearty. Amelia was soft. She looked like a southern belle who had grown old and never toughened. One somehow had the feeling about her that she had been dragged through this life and really never had any idea of how she got here."

Her brother Percy was a slightly strange man. He wasn't stupid. He had sort of an old world courtliness about him. I don't mean he was a dandy. But he had nice manners. Sissified, perhaps. No one made excuses for him. He was just Percy. His bad ride on Allah was rather the end of him. He was never the same after that.

Percy didn't know how to read. But he knew colors. And he could count. When he would go out to pick up day camp children, he couldn't read road signs. But he knew that at a red house he should turn one way or the other, and count the houses at that point. At some given spot there would be a white fence, and at the next street past the white fence there would be children on the curb with their brown paper lunchbags, waiting to be taken to camp.

That is how Percy von Ohl memorized the routes.

A few of us, on a wager, sneaked up to his room when he died. I remember that as children it struck us strange to keep urns of dead people's ashes. It was our first encounter with them. Mrs. Parker had Percy's sitting right up there on the dresser looking at us.

Most remembered him vaguely, except for the fact that he kept a pet raccoon. I recall that when Percy died, Adele and Winnona tried to take care of it but it turned vicious. And I remember that while the family had not seemed to have made much over him while he lived, it was an elaborate and beautiful service. "The Song of Hiawatha" was recited—the full version—all the way to the bitter end. And it just seemed like a fantastic tribute. It almost numbed me as a child because I had never witnessed great affection before.

"Cracks in the veneer?" asked the psychologist. "Certainly. Some of the bitterness showed through as one grew up there—some of the shallowness, meanness, humanness. She was an individualist. God, there are few of those around. I'm not protecting her but this is what I loved about her—she didn't give a damn what other people thought!

"No, I *wouldn't* live that way," she said, "but SHE wanted to live that way AND SHE DID! There are a lot of things I'd *like* to do—but I don't. Society doesn't condone .them. And I get angry with myself. This is one of the things she instilled in children—honesty... BEING YOURSELF!

"True," she added, "the floor had the accumulative dirt of years ground into it, though it obviously was swept now and then. But it was dirty. The walls were imbedded with something—heaven knows what. You could FEEL the dirt in that house. You could smell it. Couldn't *see* it, really. But it was there. It was a dirty house. Dirtier than a barn because this was human dirt.

"The house was extremely plain. It was littered, of course. They had days of cleaning, I think, when they piled everything on that round table. Some days there were piles of things; other times they were casually scattered. I think people looked for things occasionally."

Said the doctor, "I am not a fussy person. I work with three and four-year-old children and you can't be very weak-stomached and do that. Yet I could not drink hot chocolate which she had made because the pan she used would have had chile in it before the hot chocolate and hamburgers before the chile. Before that, morning oatmeal. And you could see little remnants of all of these in the cup.

"But she made her hot chocolate and did it with a flair. And served it with a flair. The cup might not have had a handle. You may have burned your hand holding it. But it was a cold night and you had hot chocolate because this is what the gracious lady did.

"Adele was not easily upset," she insisted. "It was, in fact, great fun to find one who actually openly disapproved of her world, saying that hers was an odd way to live, a *terrible* way to live. Any kind of disapproval was a flattery, an accolade. She *liked* disapproval, except she wanted you to approve of *her*.

"Her house itself," the doctor added, "was so symbolic of the life she had constructed for herself which was so empty and which was so much a shambles and so much falling apart at the seams. Yet she continued to walk through it as though she were queen of the manor—when who could possibly be queen in the kind of life she lived?

"And who possibly could be queen in a kingdom like that house was? The house was no more real to her than the life she had built around herself. She never saw it—not the way it was. What she saw was inside herself. And her people——her people whom she saw as her court jesters and her court ladies, no one else saw that way.

"But she took herself a few symbols from her early life——the people who were important to her—her southern ladies and Buffalo Bill—then found prototypes and made them into these people, whom they weren't. But that's who they were to her.

"And if there were disturbances within her household," added the psychologist, "no, she would not have stopped them by threat of ejection. She would believe in letting Nature—always Nature—take its course. Life, to her, was ongoing. She would not meddle. There was, and had to be, a dynamic continuance. . .

"You see," she smiled, "here was a person who was totally casting aside the values of the culture in which she lived and was thwarting it all by saying, 'I don't do what you do. I do things the way I do them, and this is the way I do them. If it's opposite of your way—good!'

"It seems almost a classical thing for a woman to do," said the doctor, "if she's going to reject material values, to show it in her house that she has no use for them. 'I have shelter because I'm an animal—I can't live outdoors. I must have shelter. But that's all it is. Nothing else.' She would just as soon have lived in a barn if she had been alone.

"She wouldn't be beaten. She kept going. She never quit. She had a lot to buck. That original rundown house. . . having come from gentry, or being told that she had. And told that this is what is worthwhile. And to go out there and get it! And she says, 'I'll be damned if I will!' (because she's Adele). But she goes out and tries to get something *like* it. 'I can't be that kind of royalty but I'll be *American* royalty.' "

When Adele's friend, broke, with nothing left but his elephants came to the ranch, her students swam the elephants in the river, and at least four persons who stumbled upon the scene in the Metropolitan Park river valley, swore off booze for life. The pachyderms ate her out of hay and the park commissioner came up screaming about crazy calls he got that there were elephants in his park.

CHAPTER SIX

INCREDIBLE CIRCUS

"One morning," the man across the street said, "I looked out while getting dressed and I said to Mom, 'June, what the hell is that! It looks like a buffalo!' Pretty soon here's a fellow out there putting a saddle on this huge creature and riding down Mastick Road on him, bridle and everything. I thought, 'What the hell is that!' "

The same week two fellows came down the drive with a fantastically large dog. It had been hit by a truck. She told them they could bury it right underneath where the deer had been hanging from the apple tree. And I remember when another dog crawled into her garage and had its puppies which proceeded to freeze to the garage floor. We ran into the house. "Mrs. Parker! Mrs. Parker! There's puppies all over the garage and they're stuck to the floor!"

She and the boarder, Ramona, came and saved three of them. One they nursed with a bottle for three weeks. Kept nursing it and nursing it and finally took it down to Dr. Berthold and he said it had pneumonia.

Then it died.

Buck Jones was stunt rider in Hollywood. He, too, found his way up the drive. He stayed six weeks or so and taught us all how to twirl a rope and shoot a rifle. Then the man with a trained buffalo popped in and the Leisy Beer horses showed up. Also a couple of Indian boys used to fly in and out of there in their car. A weasel from the valley had killed several ducks and she had the Indians go out and clean up all those duck remains on her porch, which was difficult for it was January and they were frozen solid to the planks. They pried them up, though, and finally wanted to eat them.

Before World War II, there was a very beautiful girl there who was a genius at riding pairs of disassociated horses, Roman style. She left to support the war effort in a defense plant, and was almost totally scalped when her hair caught in the machinery. She was always going to come back, of course, but never made it. One more spectacular individual who came out of nowhere and returned to nowhere.

And a man with an 18-year-old girl from New York lived at Parker's as man and wife, out back in a dumpy little outbuilding. The people across the street were selling an old spring mattress and hauled it out back at the couple's request, their preferring it to the cold floor. They had time to bang away on it a few nights before a car drove up with two detectives from New York, and the girl's father.

The man had crossed the state line with his daughter, dispensing with the marriage ceremony.

Parker told everybody to leave.

She ran a clean place.

Then that Harriet creature showed up with her dreaded goats. Then drunks would come staggering in and so then *they'd* be there. There'd be barn men. You'd go out sometimes and practically die of fright in the barns.

She invited Hopi Indians out there and had them set up shop in her front pasture. A whole pony troupe was out there. All the vagrants of the universe were out there.

She actually had quite a love for Indians, also, and brought out her share from the reservations. She felt sorry for them, but kept them in line. She kept tabs on them. One day she told me she kept in touch with each of their mothers.

The neighbors never did get used to their drums.

"Well, my God, that boom-boom-boom! boom-boom-boom! all night long!" explained the man across the street. "It was *awful! And*—they stayed there for a long time. About a dozen of them. At night they'd build a fire, put on their Indian clothes, dance around there, beat their goddam drums. Kind of a funny thing to hear ten miles west of Public Square.

"Of course she used them in her shows, but—gee—they must have come a month ahead of time. She had this covered wagon come out, then these Indians chased it and set fire to it. It had a paper top to it, and it was all a good show. Kids loved it. But my wife used to complain, 'My God! I wish they'd stop beatin' on them damn drums! Just that steady

112

boom-boom-boom! boom-boom-boom! just beyond the front fence.

"God!

"But I say this—the only Indian I ever saw drinkin' was the one that worked next door, the big skinny one. I found him sleepin' in the snow back of the house—like some red fallen angel or something. You know Mrs. Parker never went for no drinkin' over there. . ."

"Look!" the wife said, "I LOVE Indians and niggers but, God, they beat that damn drum *all night long! — BOOM!* BOOM! BOOM! *BOOM!* BOOM! BOOM! Those injuns used to walk out to the ranch—four or five men, maybe six or eight women and a dozen kids—a whole *herd* of 'em! Little old gray ones, medium-sized ones, fat and skinny ones. ALL DRINKIN', DRINKIN', DRINKIN'!"

Parker simply incorporated everybody into her Mother's Day Show or her Wild West saga.

The little French girl, Elena Gabriella, was at the ranch, too. She finally married and moved to New England. Her husband, a circus clown, butchered her with a cleaver, nearly severing the head. Then he wired a bomb to blow up the neighborhood, but it just fizzled and smoked and reaked and drew the police.

"How about the rodeo rider with the two kids and the pregnant wife?" asked the mailman. "He had that lovely quarter horse. 'Course the horse was laid up and couldn't be trailered and couldn't do this and couldn't do that. So where did he end up? Parker's Ranch. He comes and stays there and cures the horse and feeds it her hay. He'd promised to assist in all kinds of things to pay their freight. They lived in the trailer. They didn't pay nothin.' Parker lost $150.00. They left her with the bill for the birth of the baby.

The story of Crazy Harriet began with a phone call. A whimpering voice said, ". . . and she will just have to get rid of her goats." Mrs. Parker asked, "How many does she have?"

"Oh, I don't know how many there are."

"Well, we'll bring the horse trailer over. We can put a couple of goats up here. . ."

Mrs. Parker went over. It came out there was a goat in every empty stall and every place else and every mama goat was with goat. Honest to God, it was just one big goat thing! And this poor soul—oh, she was highly rouged, powdered— —and the deal was she could leave the beasts at Parkers until she found a place for them. She would come during the day to milk the goats and take care of them. At night she would go home.

But after dark she'd slip back. Mrs. Parker went out to the Geezle Barn one night. Here's old Harriet, the goat lady, crumpled in the hay. Mrs. Parker retrieved a blanket. She didn't send her packing. She said, "Well, you can't sleep out here without blankets."

So Harriet moved in, too.

Mary Rankin was in charge of the third barn and it was late in the month of August—and *hot*. Back by the third barn was a terrible decaying odor, something on the order of rancit lobstor. Nearby, Harriet had been given the pigpen with the little thatched roof. Mary all but took the barn apart, board by board, brick by brick, trying to find the dead animal. She was sick to her stomach working at it.

A friend and I came up from a ride and we rode back to say hello to Mary and the sudden stench struck our nostrils like a foray of putrid gas. Together we continued the search. Finally, in a pile of straw, we spied one of the hooves sticking out like a cloven pointer. One of Harriet's "babies" had died but she could not bear to bury it. So, Indian fashion, she and Spike, the hand, had put it on top of a platform and covered it with straw.

When Mary saw it, she went and told Harriet and Spike to fetch a shovel, saying, "Bury that or get off!" Well, there were so many goats it was impossible. It was finally decided to load them all up. Parker found a place for them with a man who had a goat business, putting them in a field where they could chew it down.

We started loading. He took three loads. Three horse trailer loads. On the last load, Harriet ran after us down the long gravel driveway.

"Oh, my babies! My babies!"—scratching at the trailer,

stumbling in the dust.

Then there was Dr. B——— who had kind of a problem with his mind. I mean he would awaken at three or four A.M., get into his car, motor out to Parker's, perch himself on top of a haystack and play "Blues In The Night" til the sun came up. Relieved of this strange urge at about nine or nine-thirty A.M., he would motor on to his practice from there. Sometimes he'd stay there for three or four days or a week and Mrs. Parker would take care of him. He was terrific at "Blues In The Night."

She was sitting in her kitchen the day the Russian officer walked up. His boots were shined and he was in full uniform. She asked him in and he came in. She offered him supper and he stayed and they talked. And she had him stay the night.

He put on airs but she saw through his airs. He said he had to leave the next day. She put a twenty dollar bill in his hand. He was indignant. She said to him, "Take it as a remembrance."

Four years passed. She received the money double in return. There was a letter with the money stating that the day he came to her home he was dishonest and had heavy thoughts. Then his evening with her and his talking with her turned his life completely around and he, in effect, began life again.

And the mayor showed up one day. She urged him to come in. "Now don't forget to wipe your feet! Take your hat off! Now don't catch cold! Put on your sweater!" She treated men like little boys and little boys like men. In teaching, whenever she had to correct a boy, she'd go up and put her arm around him. To girls she'd say, "LOOK, YOU STUPID IDIOT! I TOLD YOU ONCE—DON'T DO IT THAT WAY!" She could talk that way to a girl... But a boy? "Don't humiliate a little boy... things are rough enough on them."

"Oh, she was no ever-loving Brahma," assured an old veteran ranch hand. "Some people she loathed. Some children she loathed. Immediately, people she liked felt an affinity for her—these persons she would put her hand in the fire for. She had little use for phony or neurotic people. There were a

115

lot of neurotic people around her, God knows, but there's the benign neurotic and the acute neurotic. The crazy goat woman she could tolerate, perhaps because she was helpless."

Likewise at Parker's were Old Frank and Old Jack and Old Mike. Who they were or what they were, I don't know. She took out insurance policies on them. Jenkins put most of them away. Jack, at least, was cremated.

They had a home while they lived and she took care of them. Most were winos. If it took a bottle of wine a day to keep them happy—as long as they could get up to feed the horses—she'd supply it. She'd take them up to the room and let them have wine, providing they weren't unruly. Well, it was a necessity with them. One of them broke down in sobs at her casket. Somebody escorted him out.

"We had a ringside seat here," McKenna, the plumber said. "I'd come home from work. 'Well, what happened today?'—and there'd be a different story every night. The major excitement back there was the barnhands. It was funny because Manley drank the turpentine that time and they had to speed him to Fairview Hospital. The cops couldn't bend his arms, he was so stiff, and only with a heap of trouble did they eventually cram him into the police ambulance.

"The paint company said that one cupful would kill a man. Manley drank the entire pint. And two weeks later he was back on the ranch again. (He probably had worked up to it). Manley had been in the hospital ward a day or two full of fumes in his system and they were attempting to pump him out.

"His ranch friend, Fred, goes to see him there, all broken up, of course—with a goddam carton of Lucky Strikes and nearly blew the roof off of the entire east wing!"

They hired back there as many people as Manpower Incorporated sent around. They made an honest-to-God path down the drive. Every time a little wino was spotted on Mastick Road, we'd say, "Here comes another one!" Sure enough, in the driveway he'd come and on out to the back. I think that anyone coming to Cleveland looking for work, or who looked

116

like he *could* work—"right out to Parker's with ya!" You know? It was practically a rehabilitation center.

She tried to get a day's work out of fellas. She fed 'em good. Every Saturday she'd go up and bring home bags of groceries. These were for the fellows in the basement. Naturally, while she was gone, they'd sneak up to the corner and bring back two or three pints of wine. She'd come home—"Mac! Manley! Fred! Where are you!" Well, they're up in the hayloft too far gone to even be heard from. It was standard.

Periodically her boys would go on binges, careening across and falling down over their own feet. Sometimes they'd go up in the bunkhouse and the bottles would come flying out. They wouldn't leave the bunkhouse for a week at a time. Occasionally Indians rolled barrels up and down the driveway at night and other Indians did war dances. At such times Parker's Ranch was not an orderly affair and Mrs. Parker would tramp up in that bunkhouse and thrust a few of her friends out the window.

"I used to listen to these guys," Mrs. McKenna said. "One called Mac used to read the Bible all the time. He didn't like anybody, hardly. He was a steeplejack and he always talked about this country bein' better off Communist and that kind of stuff. A real agitator.

"Every one of them had something that had happened to them that had made them the ruin they were. Mac, for instance. During prohibition days, his girlfriend was walking across the Mahoning River in Youngstown—oh, he was in love with this girl! He went through this big verbal clash about it. She was stopped and shot and thrown over the bridge. After that he didn't care any more. He didn't get married. He didn't—ah, he talked *stuff* about it! I let it go in one ear and out the other.

"Then another fella, his wife passed away and he just had no interest any more, either. That was it. He had a real nice daughter out in Parma, but she figured her father was just like a bum, and he was. Then this other one—the same thing happened to him. He was in the service and he had a girlfriend. He got a 'Dear John' letter and so that was the

117

end of him.

"Well, every one of them—there'd been some derailment along the line."

"She had a lot of confidence in people," the North Olmsted chief of police said. "More than she should have had. She had the one bad habit of trying to reform people, and she was not very successful. She got herself in quite a few jams that way but I always got her out of 'em. I tried and tried to tell her not to continue that kind of stuff because she was only getting herself in trouble. She would listen to me.

"Yes sir. You're right, Chief Christman."

"She had all the respect in the world for me."

"She perked the best log coffee on the west side," smiled police lieutenant Clifford Biddulph, whose squad car knew the way to Parker's Ranch without anyone touching the steering wheel. "You could SMELL that coffee! You'd go over and they'd have a whole kitchen table down in the basement piled high with eats. There'd be five or six of her boys down there. One slept in this bunkhouse. Three slept in that one. This one couldn't get along with those. They had problems. One way or another, she managed 'em. At least nobody got killed. Occasionally we'd go over and straighten out one of her cowboys loaded up with wine. She'd go quite aways with 'em. She was a little—what you'd call—unusual. . ."

She couldn't pay many of them wages. Perhaps for tax reasons. She'd go out, though, and drop money on the ground. She'd say, "There's a couple dollars lying over there. Why don't you pick 'em up?" She fed barnhands better and more regularly than anyone. But *anyone* who required something to eat got it. It could be a kid who had just had twelve breakfasts and was hungry. . .

One of the instructors remembered Long John. He had his finger bitten off by a horse, a great big buckskin stallion. He was feeding it or talking to it and he looked and the finger was gone. There wasn't any pain to speak of, but the finger had come in handy.

"First," said the plumber's wife, "it was the kid using our phone all the time because he didn't like her listening in. Then pretty soon, 'Can you do this?' 'Can you do that?'

118

They'd come and ask Jerry to take them for wine and take them to cash checks, and Manley had to go up to the bus stop because it was raining. It was a regular shuttle service we had going!

"One day our back door was open because of the kids, I guess. I had just gotten out of the bathtub and had put on a light robe and, my God—there's Manley sitting on my couch and he's all full of horse manure; it's all over his shoes and the carpet and the couch. There he is plopped down there, half out of the picture. I propelled myself back up the stairs as if shot from a gun, to put some clothes on.

"Then I said, 'What are *you* doing here!'

"'Take me up for wine!'

"'I *won't* take you up for wine!'" Oh, there was straw and manure all through the living room—my God!

"Jerry said that night, 'This is the end, now. We're stopping it.'

"So the one day we were sitting here eating supper and the back door flies open. Thump! Thump! Thump! Thump! Fred came in and was loaded. I said, 'Jerry, there's Fred—don't kill him!' Jerry was from here to the door in one step and he was mad. He caught Fred by the shirt and simply hurled him and I didn't see Fred anymore.

"Fred knew Jerry was mad at him so he didn't talk and we didn't talk for a long time there. Then Mrs. Parker came over, asking, 'Are these fellas botherin' you?'

"Well, I mean a path was worn right through the plants and evergreens from there to here. I says, 'They seem to went an awful lot of cigarettes and things from the delicatessen.'

"She says, 'I'll stop it.'

"Then one day long after, I was downtown and I stopped in at the 25th Street market to buy some vegetables and I hear a horn honking like crazy and I thought, 'Why, that's a Good Will truck!' It was Fred. And a colored fellow's up in the cab with him. And Fred's saying, 'Boy, I see the place is changin.' He says, 'It makes me sick. God, they're tearin' down the barns and everything!'"

Then one night there occurred what has since come to be

119

termed "the cross-burning thing." The victim was Jack Clark, the negro cook, the man on the Cream of White box. Some say it was a nothing thing, that it *wasn't* what sent Old Jack packing at all. Some say contrary. No matter, the truth of the matter is that none of us kids liked Jack a helluva lot.

We thought he was pretty scary if you want to know the truth. He would go about with a meat cleaver stuck out in front of him. He'd say, "Oh, I'm not going to push this cleaver into anybody—'course if they run into *me,* I can't help *that!*"

Jack drank too much. He'd get to smashing things down in Mrs. Parker's basement. You'd hear him down there bustin' all her dishes, hollarin, "ABSOLUTELY! AB-SOLUTELY!" So the kids were scared of this guy—'specially as the years wore on when he got to drinking hard.

The kids got on a prod about Jack—and of course Mrs. Parker would never get rid of anybody. We'd come to her with some tale of what Jack had said or done. She paid no attention.

"Well, now, he's here and he's a nice man and we're not going to have all this friction, are we?"

One night the kids took things into their own hands. They decided to burn a cross out in the yard. They'd heard all about the Klu Klux Klan—oh, I don't think they *ever* would have really done anything to the fellow. They just wanted to scare him a little bit and they thought this was something very dramatic to attempt to do.

So they did it.

They put up the huge cross—with my help. We saw it all as a joke, if you must know. We put up the cross in the front pasture and lit it one night with gasoline rags.

It terrified him.

All we wanted was to fun him. We harbored no real malice. He was *part of the ranch,* don't you see?

But he was so horrified he could not speak.

Not one of us ever saw Jack Clark again.

Several hundred miles from Parker's Ranch, Mrs. Parker was to meet the English lady in the fine arts section of the

Boston Museum. Shortly before the appointed rendezvous, her purse was snatched from her hands.

She screamed.

Guards came scampering, closing the huge doors quickly, but the culprit eluded them with Mrs. Parker in hot pursuit. She tore down the street, yelling, "Stop the man! Thief! Thief!" Somebody put the brakes on him. The police came. Both the thief and Mrs. Parker rode to police headquarters in the paddy wagon. Enroute, Mrs. Parker studied the young hoodlum carefully.

"I'll wager you have not had a sandwich!"

"No'm."

She reached in her pocket and delivered a minced ham on white.

"Now, young man, you should be ashamed of yourself. That's not being prepared! *Not prepared!* I NEVER DO A THING IN THE MORNING until I first put a sandwich in my pocket. You never know what the day will bring. Be prepared! Make a sandwich! Greet the day!"

He said he would not be impartial to coffee, either. . .

She gave him ten cents.

At the bench, the arresting officer described the case to the judge and it became evident that the hoodlum had discarded her purse, keeping only the cash.

"This is regretful," the judge said. "But obviously without the purse, identification of the cash is impossible."

"That's my money!" snapped Mrs. Parker, having already lost ten cents and a sandwich.

"But PROOF, Madam, PROOF!"

"SMELL IT!" she ordered. And her lifelong habit of lining her purse with lavender scent saved the day.

The judge inhaled, grimaced, and handed over the money.

"Next case! Next case!" he shouted.

Before leaving, she sat the youthful snatcher down, lectured him, smoothed his chestnut hair, kissed him lightly on the forehead as if he somehow were the long lost wayward boy she had never born.

Writing the name and address of her ranch on a scrap of paper from her jacket pocket, she gave him the twenty dollars the judge had just handed her. She made him promise to come see her in the Spring.

But when Spring arrived in all its blossoms and fragrance and promise of rebirth, she was dead.

Many speak of Mrs. Parker driving into day camp, fresh from a recruiting mission:

"All set! All set! No problems! I just got five people—*six* people! We're all set! *All set!* No problems!"

"You have their names?"

"Oh, no—but they're coming."

"Do you have their phone numbers so we can call them?"

"No, no—they'll be here."

"Did you write down where they lived or how they'll get here?"

"No, they'll be *here!*"

(They didn't show up).

"It must have been thirty-five years ago," a woman pondered, "but I can still remember sitting on the curbstone when I was a little, little girl with my lunch in a paper sack between my knees, waiting for the beat-up old station wagon.

"In day camp we had a certain big raw-boned girl with us. The rest of us were much smaller. She was AWFULLY big and on the dumb side. We were learning how to tack western—how to tie things on a mule. This girl was told to hold the animal. She stood there holding it, tears pouring down her face. Mrs. Parker bellowed, 'What's the matter with *you?*'

"(Sob) My foot hurts!"

"Well, how come your foot hurts? *Hold* that mule!"

Finally, "What ARE you crying about!"

"The mule's standing on my foot."

"Well, get him *off!* HE SHOULDN'T BE STANDING ON A LUMP!"

At the Parker day camp, Jean Tomer was the chocolate milk and white milk lady, continually misplacing her notebook. Never had it. Was *always* writing notes to herself and losing them.

"Honey, I've ordered too many white milks. Would you

mind a white milk today instead of chocolate? (The kids probably were drinking beer back there, anyway—didn't want milk at all).

She filed everything when she could find it. When Miss Tomer left McKinley Elementary School as a teacher, her garage was filled with "Weekly Surprises" magazines——millions of them.

"If ever I go into substitute teaching," she explained, "they might come in handy."

So "Weekly Surprises" simply piled up week by week, year by year, decade by decade.

"Disorganized!" some people declared of Parker's Ranch. Parker insisted it was all to the good because "children today are too highly regimented—they need time just to plop about through the woods, suck on a piece of long grass and consider the world."

Each year Mrs. Parker set up a schedule to rake apples. Then, of course, we'd have flies by the billions. She'd take these little cross-eyed kids and give them rides if they'd clean up apples. You know kids. . . They get tired, and they'd leave the rakes and bushel baskets and you'd be falling over them for weeks. . . or they'd follow the job through—but then *she'd* not carry out her end. She'd be too busy. They'd say, "Well, I have five rides coming for the work I've done. . ." They'd never get them, and some lost respect for a little while because occasionally she didn't have time to be fair.

Also, the Coca-Cola man came and said, "Everytime I come I'm picking up fewer bottles." Of course she had to pay for them. She got spitting mad once and herded all her day campers together and told them they all were going through the valley to retrieve 347 Coca-Cola bottles! I'll never forget that because kids just kept throwing 'em over the hill year after year after year. Everywhere else in that valley the riverbed is composed of sand and shale and hard rock. The riverbed under Parker's Creek is composed of glass.

There was inevitably some new personality at the ranch each time you dared to look. Lucky, for instance. I ran into him not long ago. He's well and working for the Independent Cow Company or some place like that. Emil? I don't *know* whatever happened to him. He undoubtedly ran out of pink and red paint, his favorites.

At least these barnhands were non-violent. Just the opposite. They could hardly move. Mike's few dollars a month couldn't keep him in beer so he'd get things from boarders. Fellas would give him cigarettes and he had a talent for mooching hooch. Mrs. Parker would go out there—"Mike, have your hair cut! Mike, take a bath!" She always kept after him. Tight as he usually was, and staggering, he would try to do his work. I'd see him fall down carrying hay, pass out, sleep awhile, get up and proceed with his chores.

They all were run-of-the-mill people. Typical drunk. All but Jack. When he died, she had him cremated and carried cans of his ashes in her car for some time. I still can recall a young woman's scream when the car door opened and the cans of human ashes fell open on the road. There was even a little uneasiness among the kids at the auction, as to whether some of those cans of ashes got tossed in with the five and ten dollar baskets. . .

Mrs. Parker resented all who showed off without grounds. . . who pretended to know and in so doing, mistreated the horseflesh. On the other hand, if you had a true love for riding, showing off was permissible. You could make mistakes. She'd scream at you, but that would be the extent of it. She'd get excited when things weren't going right. Oh, she'd let off steam! She'd bawl the kids out in an effort to teach them.

She'd scream, "Yes, *what?*"

"Yes, *ma'am!*"

One neighbor had been an old driver of mule teams and horses. A slightly built man with very large feet, he worked for Mrs. Parker but also for another neighbor as a gardener. Because he had a little more money than the normal hands, he was inevitably played for the goat.

When this man got his pay, Little Johnny and Old Spike were right there on the spot. The three of 'em took off and went to town big as life. By this time the old one-time driver of mules was elderly and by the end of the night he could not make it up the driveway.

124

Wherever he collapsed in the gravel, the other two who were carrying the reserve supplies would go back to their bunkhouse, leaving him slumped where he fell. If they came in a taxi, Little Johnny would hop out one side with his bag of goodies. The driver would not understand a word he said. Old Spike would exit the other door, leaving the old man and the cab driver.

"You're home, Mac. Want to get out? Hey, Mac!"

The cab driver would knock on Parker's front door.

"Well, I have someone in the car here. They all said they live here, but one's asleep in the back seat. The other two lit out."

Parker and I went over. She pulled him out of the cab unconscious. She propped him up against a cement wall. She said to the cab driver, "How much does he owe you?" He told her. She reached in the old former mule-driver's pocket, pulled out cash, and paid the debt. The driver looked puzzled. She said with a shrug, "Just leave him lay there." Later she came back with a horseblanket.

And I've seen Old Mike, while carrying reams of hay, fall right into the rear of a horse that we knew was a kicker and a killer—and that horse would just step aside. . . fools and drunks, you know? Mike was just a little bitty guy and because he was never, ever sober, Mrs. Parker would have to lay into him.

"She's one tough old woman," he'd say over and over, low, under his breath. "She's sure one tough old woman."

A lot of people have asked how come these people never woke up with their throats cut. I can't answer it. Their doors were left open. Zombies would wander up out of the valley. I remember a man terribly bloodied and gory who came thrashing down the drive, running from men who had beaten him unmercifully.

Another time the day camp kids were getting ready to mount. Some fellow staggered up the hill in a stream of blood. He'd been bludgeoned down in the valley. His car stolen. Obviously he picked Parker's Hill to execute his escape. Mrs. Parker lived under a very wonderful lucky star.

"You think I'm kidding?" said school teacher Phyllis

Krueger, "about her being a con-artist? Look! I was madly in love with this horse 'Sis.' Dolly, Mrs. Parker's cousin, also was in love with 'Sis.' I approached Mrs. Parker and I said, 'I would like to rent Sis for a month.'

"Fine."

"I laid down the cash.

"Dolly approached Mrs. Parker also.

"I'd like to rent Sis for a month," she says.

"Same month.

"I said, 'Mrs. Parker, how is this going to work?'

"Oh, very simple! Very simple! The first one to get there!" she explained.

"Or how about the time someone called to engage thirty horses?" she giggled. "She never wrote such things in a book, but kept them in her head. An hour later someone else called—'Well, are you going to have thirty horses for us?'

"Well, of course we are!"

"But the callers were from different parties, and sixty people showed up, all restless to ride.

"Of course she got out of it (she *always* got out of it). Sixty people showed and she had thirty useable horses. Then she conned them by saying, 'Well, now, this is good! This is great! Oh, how you'll have fun, *now!* Because if you find somebody making a mistake, *you* get the horse!"

We played a kind of ballgame out there which featured a big bag made of thick sheepskin. It was played on the order of water polo, with a wooden frame with square hole at each end of the field. Someone would throw the ball in the air and it was mayhem then 'cause the only thing you couldn't do was get off your horse.

If the ball hit the ground, everybody charged in from all directions and everyone clung to the side of the horse to pick up the ball and it's a wonder we weren't all killed because nobody gave quarter. You simply charged on in and the first one there got the ball. And you could drag the kid off his horse or kill him or do anything—if he hit the ground he was out of the game.

"NEVER OWN MORE THAN YOU CAN CARRY ON YOUR BACK!" she told thousands of youngsters. She prided herself on the fact that she had lived out of a trunk all her life. Of course she had five thousand trunks, and no matter if it was an axle of an 1805 truck, it still was very precious to her and into the trunk it went.

Routine had no meaning. She would write checks and not worry about them. She would expect the bank to call her and say, "Mrs. Parker, you're overdrawn." A minute factor to her. It was the bank's responsibility to call her up and tell her they needed more money. She'd get it down. As for balancing her account, she couldn't be bothered. She had more important things to do—like going out with the horses.

If she had an appointment, it was the doctor's secretary's job to call her and remind her. She would think nothing of stopping in the middle of the road to ask a policeman directions. She could tie up traffic for ten miles. That was all right. She had to get where she was going. Those horses couldn't stay in that trailer all day!

When things upset her, she would go outside to where there was a little bit of garden. She would enjoy putting her bare feet and her hands into the soil. In this manner she boiled out trouble.

"My little boy," said the neighbor, "was a constantly frightened child. Frightened of everything. She came over one day and she took this stick and said to the child, 'IF I EVER, EVER hear you scream again!" She said, 'Now is this all right, Mrs. McKenna?' She says, 'I'm just going to use this stick on him!' And his eyes got like—he couldn't *get over it!* And it greatly helped! She was real good on stuff like that."

"She would speak to you," said the Elyria mother, "about what *you* were interested in. Show business meant nothing to me. I wasn't interested in that. But to me she would talk of nature and wildlife, the desert and the west, the mountains and animals... stories about horses and dogs and rabbits...

"I am absolutely sure she possessed a psychic quality. When I would be at some juncture—some decision-making point in time—or be seriously emotionally upset, I would very mysteriously receive a letter from her—a note at least.

"It happened on six occasions."

One can talk to strong men who were kids at the ranch. So

many generations. One fellow told a story at a reunion. He had floated on a raft in the South Pacific and there was no reason in the world why he should think of her. Somehow her words and her actions in terms of ranch days came back to him and gave him needed momentum and guts. You can multiply such stories five hundred times. We all can chart any success we've had in our lives—or peace we've known in it—to her.

A husband would ask, "How can you stand going out to a dump like that?"

The wife would reply, "You have to see her—the type of person she is. . . the wonderful good that she does. I've seen it in our own daughter. Char used to cry once in a while. She'd say, 'Mom, Mrs. Parker's gettin' old. I don't think I could ever stand to see her go.'

"I'd say, 'Now Char, all of us go some day.'

"Char is not a very sentimental person. But she would tell me how many times she would just go out there and sit and talk—of nothing in particular. . . this was the magnificent part of it. Mrs. Parker always had a way of answering indirectly. But she got her point across. Char said it helped. Sometimes you had to think a long time about a particular remark. Then all of the sudden, the answer would appear. It could be blue clouds. It could be a rainbow. . ."

"I think she definitely would make a book," assured the dentist, "purely from the standpoint that there are really so few people you ever meet in your lifetime that stick in your memory. When somebody does, you ought to look into it and find out why."

But another felt, "You can't write a book about a human being and not have them be human. But to me—she's *legend* and no doubt to my mind has proportions clearly out of bounds to what she really was.

"Yet I don't like to see balloons fall."

"Things weren't too steady around home for awhile," recalled one mother, "and I bought my son a puppy for his birthday. My mother-in-law wouldn't let him keep it. I had to get rid of the pup. Where do you take a puppy? Then I thought of Mrs. Parker.

"I remembered something she told me one time about an old man who had come out there. Some of the boys had been riding him and teasing him—'Well, he's an old drunk! He's a soak!' She said, 'I can't see this. He's just a man who needs a bunk to lay his head on. Anybody who needs a roof over his head or something to eat can come here. And,' she added, 'if you care to, go home and tell your mother-in-law I said she can GO TO HELL because she won't let your son have a pup!

"You can come out HERE. Bring your clothes."

"Occasionally," said the Elyria lady, "she'd come out here. We had a sailboat. She loved to go out in a sailboat. One day she came up the walk—'OHHHHH-H-H! ISN'T THIS A *MARVELOUS* DAY TO GO SAILING!' It was blowing up a gale. We had a Thistle—a seventeen-foot boat. I said, 'Ma'am, I can't take you out in that boat today. A Thistle is like an open bathtub. There's no deck and it'll ship water.'

"We went over to the beach and gathered shells and had a lovely time. Later we headed her out. Some of the force had subsided, much to her disappointment.

"She had dreamt of a wilder ride."

We sat for awhile. Then she remembered Mrs. Parker standing for hours wrapping potatoes in red ribbons to give as Christmas gifts, because potatoes were so high that year.

"So, no, NO, mister," she said. "You're getting nothing but sweet talk from me because I was never there when she was rude to people or when she was nasty or when she was frightening or when she was acting superior. So if I told you anything distracting about her, I'd be lying."

"The kids all had ridden Flare," said the school teacher, "and I had ridden him. He hadn't been taught much of anything. Then I sort of lost interest in Flare and another girl fell madly in love with him. For one reason or another, however, Mrs. Parker did not want this girl to ride him. She liked, in her own wily way, to match horses and people. I'd come out and this poor girl would ask for Flare and Mrs. Parker would say, 'I'm awfully sorry, Mrs. Krueger has asked for Flare.

"I hadn't.

129

"She wanted to ride Flare in a horse show.

"I'm sorry. Mrs. Krueger's riding Flare in the horse show."

"I wasn't.

"But one year at Christmas I purchased a set of Christmas cards that had a woman, a child, a dog and a horse on them. I had them printed with my name and Judy's name and Flare's name. Now I didn't own Flare. Mrs. Parker received my card. I went out there Christmas Day and she sat there at the table.

"By the way, young lady, I have a bone to pick with you!"

"She threw my card across the table.

"This is grounds for lawsuit! You're claiming something that doesn't belong to you!"

"Well—I'm sorry—I. . ."

"We sat there awhile longer. Then she said, 'Aren't you going out and say hello to Flare?'

"Oh, yes, I have carrots for him."

"There was a big bow on his stall, and an envelope. And in the envelope, a message—'I hereby give Flare to you.' "

"She came all dressed up to the voting booth," confided North Olmsted councilwoman Mary Alice Lynch, "and didn't get to vote, being twelve minutes late. I would have opened the door but I didn't have any final say," she winced. "She was SO furious, pounding on the door, screaming to us all and to God in heaven that she was a staunch Republican!

"Later on, I told her I really didn't want the job of distributing Democratic literature, but that nobody else would do it. I knew she didn't want the pamphlets, but she always cheerfully took them from me. Most everybody else made a face and closed their doors."

Two of the Parker girls had whitewashed and cleaned cobwebs not only in the first barn, but the second.

"We cleaned out stalls and took care of horses," one of them said. "Horses would come back from rides and we'd take them in—not wait to be told. We felt at home. And if you'd do something for Mrs. Parker, she so often felt she must reciprocate. 'Get ready, girls!' she said one day. 'We're going to dinner and a movie!'

"Downtown, the film was 'Train From Yuma.' Glenn Ford

was in it. On the way out she stopped at the box office and absolutely everybody knew her and pampered her. She took us to Pierre's Italian-style restaurant. She was all dressed up and just loved the waiters and the checkered tablecloths. It was nice, you know?

"She ordered the meal—spaghetti. And she said to the waiter, 'We'd like some of that real Italian wine. You know the kind I mean—the Dago Red?'"

She had a certain sympathy which I believe was quite honest, along with the theatrics and the fakery. But it was a known, conscious thing with her. She was a fake in insignificant areas which you could accept. Adele wants to show off. Who really cared? Why do all these people show horses for? Perhaps they're more reserved about it. They do it with observed protocal. Some would like to do otherwise.

They don't have the fortitude.

"You ask me all these questions," said a woman. "I prefer to simplify. Mrs. Parker was my friend. I never asked her questions nor felt I had to or ought to. See, I can enjoy *you* without knowing where you work, where you live—what you've done before, what you have, what you hope to do. I can enjoy NOW with you. And so we'd go down trail. Ride together. Maybe there'd be twenty, thirty kids. I'd ride up next to her. We'd talk about 'now'—about the things we were seeing in nature—*today. . .*"

"She was so gosh awful proud of her produce," laughed her friend, Phyllis Krueger. "I was out one winter morning when she had on nothing but a wrapper and bare feet. It was deep snow.

"I think I better go out," she said. "Those hens must have laid quite a few eggs. It's about time."

"I said, 'Wait a minute! Wait a minute! Put a coat on!'"

"It's fine weather! Fine weather!"

"She flashed across the yard through the ice and drifts, toes in. She returned. She had in her hands four of the puniest looking eggs ever created.

"Girls! Join me for breakfast. There's nothing like fresh-laid eggs!"

"She scrambled them and got out her goats milk. In fact

she tricked me on that goddam goats milk. I wanted a shot of milk to put some rum in.

"She said, 'Oh, I have lots of milk!' and she sat there looking evil.

"Are you sure this is cow's milk?"

"Certainly. Fresh, fresh, fresh!"

"Lawson's?"

"Here is the carton, my dear."

"I remained skeptical, but I wanted the milk. She won her little game. Five hours later I smelled like a goat."

With people like Parker, there is always someone willing. Her selected few—why did they stay? Because they wanted to. They jolly well complained. They did this. They did that. But they stayed on and on and on—for years. It got just short of mayhem at times. She wouldn't fill out her income tax form... she didn't keep receipts... she never kept records... she lost her money or gave it away or conned barnhands with it. We loved her, needed her, admired her, envied her—because she was truth. She was freedom. She was a free spirit.

We'd all be out there working our tails off. For nothing. Just to try to help out in the mess. She could build fires in people. Oh, God, could she build fires! In doing so, we no longer were helping her—we were helping the "situation," which of course included ourselves.

"You know who she really loved?" asked her physician. "The things that could get the best of her. Who gave her a fight. She couldn't love things that wouldn't fight her! People or animals, it made no difference. Something or someone she had to put herself out for!"

The girl in the jeans liked the memory.

"She had a group of us who were very close to her that she called 'the skunk.' And if you were one of 'the skunk,' she'd just come along and, with her fingers, would draw a couple of stripes down your back—just walk by while you're sittin' in a chair sometime. It meant that in her mind, you were up there."

The hardware man said it was her knees more than anything. She'd do this bit with Chester where she'd step on him and go straight up like a Roman candle. Real show-stopper, oh, boy! Chester was high! One night when starting her ascent, she got up to the height of his hind quarters and her foot flipped out of the stirrup. She plummeted to earth on both knees, smashing them both.

Through the years Mrs. Parker convinced everybody that her mother's ghost was around the place. She'd remark, "Well, there's *good* ghosts just like good fairies!" She believed it. Of course if you lived with the woman long enough, *you'd* believe it.

"My mother, my mother. . . this show is in memory of my mother. . ."

Everything she said and did was influenced by her mother. . .

Once at the end of a particularly hard day, assistant Mary Rankin was finished with her chores, or thought she was —and then a late rider came back in—on a white horse. Mary said later to a friend, "I just couldn't do it. I just couldn't clean that horse and I figured this was it. I put him in his stall and I went in the house. I went to bed. I was the first up the next morning in order to get at the horse before Mrs. Parker saw it. I opened the door of the stall and—stood petrified and frightened.

"The horse was snow white! I went back to the house, ashamed, and finally reasoning that Mrs. Parker somehow had discovered the infidelity and had done it herself.

"No, I didn't know of the horse," she said.

"Then, as I grew even more troubled, she bade me to calm down and not to worry. A kind of peace came over her face and she smiled slightly.

"Mother did it," she said softly, continuing with breakfast.

"I did practice teaching at Riverside School," the ranch's Phyllis Krueger explained, "and they had a social studies unit studying the settlement of the west—Indians and the trimmings. I mentioned it to Mrs. Parker and her face lit up like a theater marquee.

"Oh, God, bring them out!"

"I still was nervous about it and tried to forewarn the principal—

"Now, you know there's no plot—no plan. . ."

"I needn't have worried, Parker had the hay piled up into

tier-like seats on the barn floor. And the city kids came out. She had put Navajo blankets down to sit on. She did all kinds of things. She gave a gorgeous talk. She brought the horses over. The kids could walk around with the teacher. Two busloads of children came and went.

"If she were living today, I'd say, 'Mrs. Parker, the kids at my school have never really seen a horse.'"

"When would you like to have one there?" she'd ask.

There were the winter painting sessions.

"She did make a *head* of my $15 horse in oils," said a Parker rider, "and then I asked for his whole portrait. She looked at my horse, Flare, full in the face and said, simply, 'He's not worth it. Not worth it.' Shortly before Mrs. Parker died, I went there and Clementine the pig came galloping through the yard like a racing freight train. Flare sprang up like a lightning bolt on his hind legs, went snorting and blowing about that damned hog—snorting and blowing and raising hell. Mrs. Parker, not moving a muscle, not an *eyelash,* sitting so stone still on the mounting block, said, mostly to herself, 'Ya know. . . maybe he is worth it. . .'"

Sitting on the fence post, I loved to watch her sketch a horse. She'd begin with the bone structure and proceed to develop the whole doggone thing. It wasn't part of day camp. It was just a lot of kids interested in learning to draw, so she said, 'Why don't we have a class?' We paid her 50¢ and brought our own pencils.

"She'd come here, throw off her coat, lie down on the floor and start painting," said friend Karl Stats. "She generally used watercolor and she never had any water with her so she just licked the brush with her tongue and her mouth would be red-blue-green and everything else. This is the way she did.

"I found I could *enjoy* her pictures," confessed Stats. "Now my son's an artist and has taken many prizes. There's one of his masterpieces on the wall. To me, it belongs out in the barn someplace. But to an artist, that's a good picture. What do you think it is? It's a bunch of coolies burying a bird. This is what it's supposed to be. It won second prize somewhere. To me—*nothin!*

"Now Mrs. Parker would paint a horse and you could tell

it was a horse.

"My personal feeling is that Van Gogh and some of those other fellas never were artists. They never could paint. That's why they painted these distorted things. To me, if you have a calendar, get the picture, frame it, put it on the wall—it's *your wall! You're* going to look at it! That's what you like! And to heck with the other guy, because that's just about what these artists tell you.

"I tell my boy, 'Then why not sell all your stuff to *artists?* Why go out and look for some sucker to buy it?'

"Mrs. Parker. . : now she could paint a horse. . ."

Newspaper writer Hulda Lesher had no problem with Mrs. P.'s occasional combat with reality.

"I don't believe she made too much up," she smiled. "Not really. . . She would embellish life a little if it were too gray. With Mrs. Parker, nothing could be a lie. She took the truth and planted daisies around its base and served it to all of us. She had a thousand personalities with which to deal and the truth would be served one way to one, another way to another.

"No. . . accuracy wasn't her strong point, but it wasn't the *circus* strong point, either. The emotions. . . entertainment. . . care nothing of truth. Illusion is the appeal to what seems to be and what we would like to have been. . ."

Quoted the newspaper, "There is something in her of the grande dame, something of the pioneer, something of a morning white sun spilling light across a meadow and something of a gypsy. Nothing that accident has tossed up on an addy of wind, nothing that trouble has blown in flattening blasts has found her harassed, nor entangled her firm balance. This is a curious scene to the stranger who might wander in for directions, find himself staying for dinner and coming back the next day to mow the front field. . ."

"Oh, my, I KNOW you won't believe this, sergeant!" the frantic neighbor shouted over the telephone. "But, oh, I swear to you, there's an ELEPHANT trying to get in my door and it came from PARKER'S RANCH!"

"Yes, lady, sure. Now just go to bed, we'll take care of everything. (Oh, boy, we got another one, Harry. . .")."

135

ADELE AND PONCHO

Mrs. Parker's love affair with the news media began with her arrival in Cleveland in 1929. Stuck there with her Palace Theater booking cancelled, with seven horses, 70¢, and a rabbit to her name, she made the first of hundreds of phone calls to reporters, announcing "a famished giant drinking a chocolate soda in the Mall Drugstore!" It turned out to be only her rabbit, "Poncho." The story appeared anyway.

CHAPTER 7

RABBITS IN THE OATMEAL

(Parker's Ranch Journal)

January 8: 3PM Mrs. Ruth—Sunday school group from St. Peter's Church, between 20-25 people for hayride @ 75¢ per person. . . cocoa and wieners for supper.

January 9: Bell Telephone will call. 10 couples. . . will send deposit.

January 10: Mrs. Arthur O'Harris—call 1:00 P.M. Two boys, eight and nine, have a hound dog. Live near John Marshall High School. . . Mr. and Mrs. Howard Delph in cottage.

January 11: Pups are four weeks old: Muffet, Sweetie Pie, Champ, Judge, Vickie and Precious.

January 12: Mrs. Paul C. Ruth, Bo. 0204, did Flying Dismount and got stepped on. . . Her daughter asked about sleigh ride. Call when it snows.

January 14: Woman dropped by with cub scout son—YUK! AGHh-h-h!

January 15: 20 people want to use kitchen for weiner roast.

January 16: Little Fashion died after midnight—choked from a grain of corn in windpipe. . . fought all night for her breath.

January 17: Have one car at Harding Jr. High School. George—call this number to reach your mother: ME 2991. Ask for the lady upstairs. . . Call C.N. Davis at the Lion's Club.

January 18: Millie not here today—turn the monkey out. Call Mr. Kilband about carriage for the March 17 parade... Mary in town for music lesson... 3:30 P.M.—Horace Mann group, maybe... Somebody pick up cake at Herman's Bakery at Kamm's Corners. 8PM Parker's Ranch dinner—18 coming.

January 19: Saw "Fighting O'Flynn"... See Mrs. Allonso about the manure but check the price... Straw (wheat) $15.00 a ton, delivered.

May 8: Horse show today. Beautiful day. Sun warm. Apple blossoms. Big show—lots of people. Thankful for all blessings. Lovely roses from Parkers Ranchers.

May 23: Telephone bill of $70.65 due.

May 24: Earache today... Mrs. Calvert wants covered wagon for display for two days... 2 hr. lesson for Miss Winkels... Girl Scout group coming—15, 16 riders... Donna Mac Farland wants kitten... Man wants two ponies and attendant at NACA picnic grounds—$15.00... Goldfish Army and Navy Store called—new Army blankets arrived... Kay wants refrigerator—home any day but Thursday.

December 30: On my desk—
telephone
horse statue and clock
Roman horsehead book-end
picture in standing frame of Chester & Daisy (my fine horses)
long black box of pencils
long tray of inks
pin coillon
George Hanover shoe tree
an American flag
one pair of horse snippers
one blacksmith's hammer

one Life Magazine
my black pocketbook
one shoe brush
box of Copenhagen snuff
letter cutter
2 ink wells
books on horsemanship
& this day book.

January 5: Snow just covered the ground. Bright sunny day—wee bit cold. Cancelled all riding. Parker's painting horses... Gabbie & Curley left here for South America. All things under control. Nona sold a puppy.

January 6: Chickens hatched in truck—okay. Cow re-bred third time... Have all rubbish removed from yard. Came and got covered wagon for Music Hall and barbershop quartet. Will not need team. Can Parker talk to Lakewood High art club on March 1st?

April 8: Cold and snow. Big day—60 kids coming. No more egg reservations—full house. 3PM to 5PM. Hayride & Easter egg hunt.

June 1: Overnight ride—bring flashlights, white lanterns, first-aid in saddle pockets, canteen, water jugs with water, stickers on your saddles, coolers for the hot horses, knife in saddle pocket, steaks, bacon meat, bedrolls, green tarp that is in covered wagon, rope, can opener, knives, forks, spoons, case of Dad's Rootbeer, fruit juice, milk, coffee, sugar, canned milk, eggs, cookies, flour, lard, baking powder, sweet stuff for hotcakes, mints, carrots, green onions, mounting block, feed, tarps, tent trailer, picket line... Mrs. Hook asks for Big Red and 6 other horses "not too frisky and not too tame."

August 30: Wild West Show rehearsal. Sleep-out tonight. Get Kleenex, cold cream, leg make-up, war bonnet, beard at Masons Costume.

November 2: First snow. Colder than Greenland. Everything froze. Arrange for breakfast in valley. Team and green wagon. Return by noon. Jelly, bacon, eggs, hot cakes, coffee, fruit juice, syrup, cream, gravy—12 people.

November 3: Hen layed an egg. Black cat killed by cow. Hay 75¢ a bale at H.T. Howard's, Rt. 1, Valley City. Parker in bed all day with cold. Mary has hair appointment.

January 10: Order 2 tons of Kentucky slack. Judge, our Pomeranian, at Barnes Hospital with distemper. Killed chicken with rifle today. Saw a man stand on one finger. "Wonderful Chief" born in August, 1932. Yellow comb and gold lipstick on top of towel cabinet in kitchen belong to Naomi Loehr. Her sister will pick them up tomorrow.

June 6: Mule to stand in front of Hotel Statler all day. Mr. Schmunk will call to ok.

August 24: Cherry very sick. Pick up Judge at Dr. Barnes. Circus on North Olmsted parkgrounds—fire department added. Taft School 6PM to 9PM. Pony ring and ropes. Can fire inspector drop by to discuss fire detection? Mr. Court may want covered wagon today and tomorrow for scenery at picnic.

September 27: Parker was judge at Chagrin Valley show. Mary will be away after 4 o'clock. Rolls, ice cream, salad, catfood.

September 28: Joe Feldkircher to rent back pasture for picnic—28 people. Creative Arts Club. St. John, our hand, arrested in Fairview. $25.00 waiver.

140

January 27: Helen's slip is in front hall... Vitamin pill in cupboard. Mrs. Parker's strap from Mr. Worthington... Eggs, bread, butter, straw, corn. Mrs. Jofka, Shady Road, Olmsted, has stud horse for sale—6 years old, white, with blue eyes.

May 13: Remove things on barn floor. Remove lumber from cabins. Fix fence between orchard and campus. Fix crate. Fix drinking fountains. Get locks for tank. Paint cars. Paint hay wagons.

November 26: My black rabbit died—my lovely little rabbit.

December 29: San Jose jumped the gate—fell on his back and hurt himself... Evening at Phyllis's.

May 20: Group of nursery children coming for an hour—no riding—just to look around.

June 10: Joseph Burns hauled mules to Musicarnival. Somebody owes him $20.00.

July 3: Magic had to be put down... broken muscle and could not give birth. Dear Magic—she was the *best* cat—we loved her for her real self and her lovely kittens... She had her troubles, brave little cat.

July 27: Buffalo Bill's boots to go back to shop—also Indian top shirts go back for drawstrings.

July 30: Joe Herringer is looking for a van that can be sold or rented to Cyrus Eaton to haul the Troiks and three horses.

September 2: 1 pt. of oil of tar
2 qt. linseed oil (raw)
1 qt. kerosene
1 dose of 2 oz. twice a day for horse cough

141

January 22: Must pay November phone bill by today! Call workmen about roof blown off third barn. Sandra Rollin. . . could come by bus. . .*wants job*. . .could answer phone but doesn't want to do dishes. Illuminating Company man promised hay ride in payment for pole. Alligator will be here.

March 21: Davis bringing antelope meat for dinner. Ramona, please order rabbit pellets. Harry Forwood, Manger Hotel, called about renting a white horse for a Hanna Theater play in three weeks. Quoted $15 per performance for 2 wks or $240.

October 22: Walter, call Ginny. "Bandit" needs shoeing right away.

January 21: Eugenia had a dream of being in a cave. Someone rolled a big rock across the opening and all died.

February 15: Like first day of spring at ranch. Saw one robin and hens laid first egg of the year.

February 16: 4 eggs.

February 18: 2 eggs.

March 3: Whitey did not come home. He said he would come home in time to do his night work. It is now 9PM and no Whitey. But—I cleaned and bedded the horses and helped Eugenia feed.

June 15: Whitey called—said he was going a long way off and had only 75¢

June 17: Whitey's at the draft board.

January 1: Keep desk clean. Answer all mail. Be kind. Keep well. Plan ahead. Have faith and love.

April 16: Tom got Howard's car. Got home drunk. Police came.

May 12: A perfect day. Great crowd. Everything went well. Everybody happy. Thank God and everyone else!

Toward the end, Mrs. Parker had to stand on the picnic bench to mount a horse. Arthritis and heart. All of us pondered what it must have been like for her—these early warnings of Eternity. It must have been crushing to have to give up. To have to say, 'I can't do it anymore,' though she did it long after anyone else could have done it.

Remembers rider and horse-owner Sue Neneman Wendt, "The riding club asked her to talk about horses so she told them about 'me and my accomplishments and things that happened in England.' She acted things out. She whinneyed like a horse. She pawed and stamped and shook her head. This was Mrs. Parker and I loved this and I was never, never embarrassed or felt funny. Strangers were flabbergasted to learn that she really was like this—the strangest, warmest character I ever met."

Laughed Sue, "She always, *always* got sidetracked in her talks. Groups did not ask her back. She got off on tangents. But I enjoyed them time and time again—the 'horse on the railroad track story' and the ghost stories. . . But—for *most* people, it was sheer eccentricity.

"People laughed and giggled and scoffed. It seemed to egg her on. She increased her tempo and her volume—more pawing the air, more whinneying, more kicking wildly with the legs, more loud snorting of nostrils. . . I enjoyed it because this was *her*.

"And I loved her.

"Perhaps it happens to many with age; they become the butt of jokes and are rebuked and time and time again made to feel embarrassed. Yet for those who knew them and loved them at an earlier time, they can see the progression and understand what is happening now, and sometimes close their eyes to the sadder parts of it. Perhaps there *is* a time when you should quit going out and talking publicly but she

143

couldn't quit. She always said, 'If you quit, you might as well just quit completely.' "

"On the contrary," sighed the women's club member, "I believe she exercised the world's greatest put-on simply because she *enjoyed it!* Causing her audiences to wonder... and feel uneasy... and check for the exits. This was her *brand* of impishness. I'm sure she was way ahead of everyone else. I used to watch her and she'd do this with people she thought were phony. She may have thought these women's groups were a little for the birds. 'What do they want me to do—come out and *perform?* Well, they'll *get* a performance!' "

"She was not alone very much," her doctor said, "yet I'm sure she had lonely times. She took 'today' very well and enjoyed it. She was glad to see you. When she asked you how you were, she truly wanted to know. If she said to a kid, 'What are you doing in school?' and the kid said, 'I hate geography,' she wanted to know why he didn't like geography and what was he studying in geography and what was the matter with it?' "

Once she had a little exhibit in the Sportsman Show basement and she grabbed hold of my hand and just talked to me and talked to me. Years later she seemed different somehow. More withdrawn. A strange look in the eyes.

Sometime in the last decade of her life, she was approached in the dead of winter by the agent of a scandal magazine who paid her one hundred dollars to advertise his wares on the sides of her covered wagon. This, for her, became part of the price of independence. She draped the old vehicle with the advertising cloth they had made up for her—it played up all the pulpy scandals—and she drove the wagon downtown every day for a month. Parker's Ranch was glad to see cuts of bread in winter. She would realize this. The public wouldn't.

Still, the always-present, never-ending swarms of the young crowded about her. They hung on her every word. They virtually *lived* there and she virtually had to *push* them through school. She'd say, "You go to school, now—and you *graduate!* All her children. It was an awful fight. But where else could they find Indians. . . *real* Indians? One man from Brecksville said, "I heard th' noise fer twenty miles! I come over t' see what it was. WOW! What a western show THAT was! I sat there crying the whole time!"

Mrs. Parker planned for yet another show after her bad heart attack. She kept saying, "Come over," and Eugenia kept going around and telling everyone, "Please, don't anybody show up! She's not *supposed* to do this!" So nobody came.

Parents and friends of Parker's Ranch weren't too nuts about all that transpired there in the later years, yet it did not stop them from pitching in; from helping to keep her little show on the road; from saving Parker's from total and absolute economic collapse. It was something she wanted to do, so everybody just—went along. . . The show had to go on. It got to the point, somehow, that you were very sure this is what drove her. If Mrs. Parker had had to sit in an old folks home, she would have been pathetic. She desired to be out front, leading this thing. She had to, and if you loved her enough, you helped her lead it. Even if it wasn't the biggest—or even any *good*—in her eyes, it might be. She knew it really wasn't, just as we all knew. But she would build it up so she could talk about it and make you think it was the most beautiful thing that ever happened.

It was during this period she said to Jackie Loehr, a promising teen-age equestrienne, "Get your education first, Jackie. You can always come back and ride horses. Don't just get out of high school and throw yourself to the horses because unless you're from the rich area where they can afford to put you through and set you up on the right beast, you're never going to be all that special on the horse show circuit. No, it's your schooling that's going to get you the job that will give you the position and meaning in life. Get your college education first—*don't stay here!*"

"And I was horse-crazy enough," said Jackie Loehr, "that if she had said, 'Will you stay and help me for the rest of your life?' I would quickly have answered, 'Please, may I?' "

"Whan I got a bit older," said another girl, "she used to warn me about guys. This might seem vulgar to say, but she was talking to me one day... she didn't really have much to say about a male... except she said one thing—and she stressed this very much—she said, 'Don't ever let a man feel your breasts.'

"I don't know why she stressed this like she did. But in my talks with her, this was the only point she kept repeating. It just stuck in my mind as kind of funny. I—I can't say why—well, I was young. About sixteen, but I couldn't see why she would say that so much..."

She talked individualism to the circus rider:

"Her favorite word—'dignity.' If you can be nothing else," she said, "be dignified. And she'd tell us girls, 'Don't ever let a man do anything to you that you can't turn around, look him in the eye and tell him to go to hell!' "

She possessed, the psychologist believed, a unique sense of freedom.

"She didn't put people or animals in cages. Even if you were going to do something hurtful to yourself—if you said, 'Mrs. Parker, what do you think of this?' she'd tell you the pros and cons, tell you what your chances were of being successful—not just horses, now—but in life... She'd tell you her opinion, her feeling, her belief... tell you both ways you could go. She wouldn't try to con you. There were exceptions—but she had reasons when she entered into manipulation. Usually you weren't aware that you'd been had, but if you were had, it was for good reason. It helped build your character."

For one to imitate the rationale and lifestyle of this lady, one could well assume close friends and followers, also enemies and critics:

"One of the kids had a quarter horse named Peanuts and I was riding this animal in the pasture across the street, and she pulls out and yells, 'You get OFF that horse and *get off right now!*' " squealed a raging neighbor.

"Now mind you!" howled the woman, "I'm a *woman* and I didn't even know her hardly at all. And she yells it again—'AND YOU GET OFF RIGHT NOW! YOU HEAR ME? THAT HORSE IS *NOT* FOR YOU!'

"Well, Christ Almighty!

146

"I say this truthfully," bitched the woman, "something about Adele Parker did not strike a chord note. I just never liked her. I knew I *couldn't* like her. Something over there simply was not right. I'm saying how I *felt,* now. She never appeared to care if she talked to me, though she would fall out of the car to blow at my husband. Let ME be out there at the mailbox, so help me God, she would wear blinders.

" 'Oh, didn't see you, my dear.'

"That also went for her little brood."

Said the Hungarian woman, "Arthur and Osler K——— were a famous Hungarian circus family. Mrs. Parker said he was the finest high school dressage man in the country. He had the same opinion of her. He was a different sort of man. He had the Lippazoners. Eight of them. He got them from Jungle Smith, a millionaire in Illinois now trying to make it in the big league social scene. So he had these horses and he was making a Spanish riding school unit to go on the road.

"I didn't like him. I thought he was a dirty old man. He really was. He was in his 70's and he was always on the make. I didn't like the way he worked with his horses, either. He'd given them sugar but then he'd come in so hard with the whip. . . so I talked with Mrs. Parker on the phone.

"I finally called her because he was going to take me and I couldn't stand him. Mrs. Parker said, 'K——— drank the very best scotch, the very best Napolean brandy, the whole bit. And he always dressed in his riding clothes, was *most correct. . .'*

"But he wasn't a very nice man.

"He was a dirty old Hungarian."

"I remember her shows," the businessman recalled, "good *kids* shows. . . 'We're puttin' on a little show for the kids!' All of the sudden who's out there but Parker in an act. There was NOTHIN' she loved more than to be in front of the people and get the big hand. Her sister was the same. First thing you know, here are the two of 'em out there—you're waitin' for your *kid,* you're sittin' here in the dust to see your *kid* perform—and out rides Mrs. Parker.

"I *knew* Mrs. Parker was a good rider. That she could do anything on a horse. Even the impossible. I wanted to see what some of those *kids* could do. But here was Parker out there. She couldn't RESIST this. She had to get out front and collect the big hand.

"Youngsters inevitably brought her roses and she wept over them. But it was all programmed—planned by Parker herself before the show. Kids wouldn't tell their mothers that. They just went home and said, 'Well, we're chippin' in and buyin' flowers for Mrs. Parker.'"

"For the fifth straight week, part-time, I started fixin' something up," the mechanic explained. "A person come along and said, 'What are you doin' that for?' I said, 'Oh-h-h, come on, *somebody's* got to help Mrs. Parker!'

"Well," came the answer, "she's had somebody all her life. When you're through, she'll have somebody else."

"I said, 'What do you mean?'

"He said, 'She's just using you.'

"Now I'm not sure if she looked at it that way," the mechanic said, "but, frankly, that is what Mrs. Parker did."

"My last encounter with her was when the children were small," said the young mother, "just after we left Colorado. Linn was three at the time. She'd ridden a horse for a year in the West and I was anxious to show her the ranch where I grew up. Parker was particularly bitter that day. I hadn't been back for years and I'd asked for one of her horses for a half hour—bareback. I can recall her yelling at the three-year-old, and then at me because of some infringement the child was committing. She seemed just to be having one of her flare-ups again. But it stuck with me.

"I never went back."

"The part," the girl said, "I remember the most was that my father had been drinking a lot, and she tried to step in and instruct us—that we should accept it, not fight it. . . just go along with it. At the time I rebelled against this. I mean I figured it was none of her goddam business. . ."

"We are in the horse business," the trainer said. "I'm interested in the horse part, not the wild west part. So many people looked at fond old Parker's Ranch and took it as it was; and when they left Parker's their horse life ended. They could afford to look back and weep and romanticize. Others of us had to go on in competition with the rest of the world, and in that respect you could not even afford to be associated with Parker's Ranch in competitive horsedom of today.

"You see," he asserted, "there's never been a good horse come from Parker's. They never made a horse, never made a rider, yet professed to do so many things. Ironically, in Parker's own circle, they all were champions. Outside it, they were doggy diddle. You just never told people you were from Parker's Ranch because if you did, the minute you stepped into that ring you were considered another of those characters on one of those goddam dumb horses. . . even the judges would just turn their heads and wait for the thing to get out of the ring."

Then the letter arrived from Karl K. Granger of Poland, Ohio, ready, at 84 years, to defend her genius and character at any cost:

Dear Mister:

Regarding your letter of no date about Mrs. Parker, I surely would like to be in on that. I saw her as a guest artist in Ringling's Circus right in front of the grandstand with her long hair, Stetson hat, fringed coat, on a great big bay horse, doin' all those things that Arthur Godfrey does with his Lip horse. . . but a greater act than his on account of her age (70).

They shut down all three rings while she performed right on the track by the middle ring and she got a grand ovation. I had gooseflesh and resolved to meet her as I am a veteran horseman 84 years old right now.

So I went and found her aluminum trailer and approached her where she was sitting under the fly canopy while her fine old barn hustler was working on her horse. I gained audience by telling her how enthusiastic the full-up grandstand was about her and I got further hospitality, a seat at her little trailer.

I reached in the pocket and showed her some snapshots of my pinto horse Rocky (whom I had to put away last spring at 27 years on account of paralyzed hind quarters), but a legend in this town of Poland, Ohio, as I had ridden him 360 days of the year for 13 years, across and around this village,

149

and hundreds of kids—some now in high school and college—have sat on him.

My friend Kilcawley had known her at one time and he was enthusiastic about booking her, which he ordered done. I watched for her to arrive which she did at noon on a swell hot day pulling her horse in an aluminum trailer, hopping out of her car fearing for that animal. I went up to her and she excitedly wanted to know her barn, saying she hoped it would be one of the old stables under the trees.

I went to the office which could neither locate the barn nor comply with my request to appraise Mr. Kilcawley of Mrs. Parker's arrival and her heat-struck animal. Seems he was in a director's meeting and against their protests I walked right into the meeting and whispered the situation into Mr. Kilcawley's ear. He jumped up and hurried out to Mrs. Parker and greeted her like a long lost wealthy aunt and she was just as cordial, being somewhat overwhelmed by Kilcawley's greeting.

She cast off her frown, straightened her fringed jacket, stood as erect as an Indian brave, and acted her real self, which, if these words will do, I'll say she looked every inch the dowager queen of all horsewomen for which, indeed, she was.

For God bless her, may she have horses in the Great Beyond, of which I wish to take occasion to declare I am a great believer. If someone says there is no God or life hereafter, I mean to ask them, "How do *they* know?" And so, Mrs. Adele von Ohl Parker, hail to you up there and all us horsemen and horsewomen will hang together and aim to be present at the big round-up.

Hold everything!

Karl K. Granger

veteran horseman, coon hunter, one-time amateur baseball catcher, one-time Boy Scout leader, long-time churchman, 50-year salesman, 50-year Mason, one-time special deputy sheriff, assisting the Department of Justice in rounding up Reds.

150

P.S. Must tell you I saw Buffalo Bill's show several times.
He once spoke to me personally. He shouted, *"Get out of there!"*

In 1955, Mary Jester Allen, niece of Buffalo Bill and curator of the Buffalo Bill Museum in Cody, Wyoming, wrote to Adele Parker, the first the two had corresponded in thirty-eight years. Mrs. Allen was gathering mementos for this famous American showplace. Following is Mrs. Parker's response—one of her most expressive communications:

My dears—
Friends indeed!
How did you ever find me since 1917?
Like you I have been collecting things from Revolution days—
Thinking of what I may have that would be of value to you: An old pony express saddle like on the Christmas card; an old bucking horse saddle—high fork and cantlo—beautifully carved, good condition like Belknap rode High Tower in... a Mexican saddle—cut through, carved most handsomely... no stirrups... my Mother's sidesaddle that my sister rode in the show—it was bought in Wyoming in 1893—fine shape.
Have some old bits and spurs, bridles, hair and rawhide... Have some Indian beadwork, blanket strips of Iron Tail's—did have his headdress... Have some old photos and some Indian pictures.
Mrs. Decker of Denver, the Colonel's sister, had a painting of me by Schreyvogel where I am reaching for my six-gun—kneeling on a horse lying down. She told me that when the colonel left the Irma Hotel the last time he took five paintings with him and the one of me was one of them.
Wasn't I proud!
Long time I have been wanting to keep the name of Buffalo Bill alive and loved. He was the Father of the West. Have hoped that I could put on a show—to play where he played... a very small show but good stuff... to make enough money to pay for a statue in bronze—or a picture—to

be put in every library... NOW IT COULD BE DONE—to make a memory drive for the museum.

"The Spirit of Buffalo Bill!"

I put on a performance here—for the high school—marvelous success! —a 1½ hr. show on the high school track. It could be done on the stage like our old vaudeville act except make it a full program or something... Think it over—I have the horses and know-how to do it...

Where is Wayne Albee, the photographer of Seattle or Tacoma, Washington? I do want to know so very badly.

Have a picture of the Colonel cutting his birthday cake.

Guess I am about the only living relic after all with spirit of real showmanship from the old school, and I have made good use of it—thanks to the Colonel!

I have 60 horses and I am in great condition—ride harder now than ever. I am alone—and am very comfortable and happy—with a wonderful business. But I would be happier if it would mean business for both of us to do all I can for the museum.

Love and best,
Adele von Ohl Parker

She motored right out to Cody, Wyoming, to deposit a car full of memorabilia at the front door of the Buffalo Bill Museum. She visited, while there, Mr. Fred Garlow, the grandson of Colonel William Cody. He said of that visit, "She had heard I had an original Edison film of my grandfather's show of 1907. Of course there was no peace until I brought it out. I began showing it to Adele at six o'clock in the evening. At a quarter to two in the morning we were still at it. She said, 'Show it again, Fred! Oh, God, show it again!' She'd push up to the screen each time and shout, 'Here it comes! Oh, watch it now!' And each time Mrs. Parker on film would come charging out under a full head of steam, swoop down at a gallop, and scoop up the handkerchief!"

Did Adele Parker spend the last of her life waiting for the stage coach to return?

"Those times," said a friend, "when things were quiet,

152

when there was no noise, no activity, she'd delve into her theater trunk and pass around a few clippings. Some say everything she did, everything she said, everything she *was* was a re-creation of the past—digging it up and serving the bones. . ."

"Well, that was her life, honey," said another. "It was horses and Indians and guns and shooting—screams in the night, for God's sake!"

"Oh!" offered the doctor, "*every* incident today was an incident from 25 years ago or 50 years ago. Every person was a person from half a century back. If she hated you today it was because she hated somebody like you then. She never stopped wooing around that revolving bulletin board. She never came out of the Wild West Show. Not ever!"

Once you have had your name in lights and have seen your picture life-size on Broadway, it is impossible ever to be normal again. Rarely did she drop a remark about how she went downtown and nobody knew her. Or she went into a restaurant and wasn't recognized. This hurt. She seldom mentioned it. But at one time wherever she would go in town, someone would rush up for her autograph or picture, saying, "Miss von Ohl, aren't you playing the *Hippodrome* this week?"

"Adele," the psychologist reasoned, "had built herself this little court and was very much afraid by this time that if she did too much, her own position would become precarious. Nor would she sacrifice her kingdom for her sister. You see, Adele was hard on herself and she was hard on others. She wouldn't expect Winnona to complain of the grossest disrespect or lack of attention. Why would she? *Adele* wouldn't. This is the way it was.

"She built her whole life on a dream that she kept pretending was reality. Particularly late in life, she didn't dare to shatter it with discipline or bullheadedness in her home. She couldn't take the chance. It was too late. The whole kingdom could collapse. The whole dream. It never was, of course, and what doesn't exist at all, one is terribly afraid of losing."

The year is 1935. Mrs. Parker and her trick horse, "Daisy," practice a routine. "Daisy" is shown making a series of jumps using only its hind legs—a trick Mrs. Parker taught her to do when when she rode for the Ringling Bros. & Barnum & Bailey Circus.

CHAPTER 8

RIDING TO PARADISE

"Mountain Rose," the woman smiled, "was my favorite. I lay awake nights wondering if I'd get that horse. Oh, I've *got* to get that horse!"

"But coming from a suburban town, I would be last again. Somebody else would have her. And Mrs. Parker, who called me Curly, would say, 'Good morning, Curly, how are you? Which horse do you want to ride?'

"I don't care, Mrs. Parker."

"One day she had a boy on Mountain Rose. He had already mounted and was so smugly confident of a long morning's ride. In an instant she saw my face. I wasn't any good at hiding things.

"She said to him, 'Which side of the horse did you get on?'

"The left side."

"Well, how about if you *had* to get off on the other side, what would you do? *Show me!*"

"He gestured and said, 'I'd get off this way.'

"Let me see you do it."

"The kid got off on the wrong side."

"*NEVER* GET OFF THE HORSE ON THE WRONG SIDE! Okay, Curley, you take the horse."

"I went on the ride," she continued—"fifteen, twenty of us—in painfully cold weather in November. We crossed the river at Little Cedar Point and the water gushed and slammed along its banks. One fellow in crossing was dumped from his mount. He fortunately hung on through the impossible current. He was dragged across.

"But by then it was too far to go around the roads to get back home. He'd have froze to death. Mrs. Parker said, 'Get back on that horse, give me the reins!' The two of them went back. He could never have crossed the river again alone after being dumped. She took him back across the water, shouting, 'Head for the barn!'—then reversed her animal and charged back across to us again, through the raging frothy current.

"She was rough

"Another time," she laughed, "we were ready to ride in the middle of a sweltering mid-afternoon. Two great trucks pulled in. Adele stopped everything, had us bring the horses back, water and feed them. When we returned, she was still marveling over some free telephone poles she had gotten. She was going to build a new fence with them. 'Oh, my telephone poles are here!' she exclaimed, and stood there clapping her hands."

Ah, those overnights—those horrible things. She separated the girls from the boys. She'd lie down, the boys on one side, girls on the other. Her head was down, a dog on each arm. We knew she slept three winks and was up. You couldn't stir. She dozed always with one eye open. No trouble with morals in the valley. A little smooching when you could get it, but a clean crowd.

From these excursions we would return exhausted. Mrs. Parker would retire to her room—and *that* would be all of Mrs. Parker. That would be it, because nobody else was *allowed* upstairs. Poor Mr. Neneman, the high school art teacher and Parker's camp counselor, remained downstairs. The phones were out (the phone bill had not been paid again), and there were, to say the very least, a huge pile of children to be disbursed.

What could he *do* with them at eleven o'clock at night? He didn't know where they lived. He didn't know how to contact the parents. One night he went up and pulled all those women out of their beds.

"Come down here and take care of these kids!" he demanded.

"Now, Albert, *someone* will take care of them."

That was Mrs. Parker.

On one night sojourn through the woods and thistles, a fellow named Vance was elected to kill the chickens for the evening meal. I held the little bastards while he beheaded them. Due to the dullness of his axe and the general dullness of Vance, I didn't care to dine that evening. I recall we had nothing but rain the whole time. Also, the horses got loose from the picket line and two fellows decided to leave the campfire and retire early.

They proceeded to undress in their tent, forgetting about the lantern behind them. They put on the most incredible shadow show for the whole campfire. Millie laughed so hard they had to carry her away.

Mrs. Parker wore a long black nightshirt that was never long enough. Still she'd go make her rounds of the sleeping bags, tucking the little ones in. And always on the trail she took her daily bath—in a barrel.

You'd go out on an evening ride, tie the horses and build a fire. Ma'am would have hunks of meat she'd throw into the flames. First time you witnessed it, you thought, "Oh, my God!" but she'd be so proud, so energetic, so eager!

"Ready for yours, my dear? You want it rare? Well done? Medium?"

She'd bring it out covered—saturated—buried—with coals and gray coal dust. You'd look at it.

"What do I do with this?"

"Just take bread. Scrape off the black. Chuck it in your mouth."

She would rig this three-day ride where we'd take two pack horses, Pinto Girl and Old Spot. She kept repeating all the while we were packing up, "Now the one thing we can't forget is the rattlesnake rope!" She explained how important it was. "You must lay it around the campsite to prevent rattlesnakes from reaching you, for fear of the hemline."

That night Mary Beth rode Grey Dolly who was blind in one eye and who would attack you for the pure joy of it. Mrs. Parker would therefore take a bell along to string on Dolly in case she got loose and for fun's sake decided to cave in our ribs as we slept. It was dark when we slid down the hill to the spot she had chosen to make camp. We'd forgotten only two things—the bell and the rope.

On an overnight ride—"Raincoats! Do you have your raincoats!" We would hide them in the load that was to be *driven* to the campsite. One night we got soaked to the skin and she just had no pity on us—she made us keep right on going and catch cold because we all had disobeyed and stuffed our rain gear in the truck, which never showed up. There was a lesson every ten minutes. It didn't have to be about horses.

"One night on our ride to Strongsville," a young woman recalled, "it got dark early and she shouted, 'Prepare to make camp right here!' We tied the horses up and started to get ready for bed when the 17-year locusts hit, causing considerable shrieking and screaming.

"Locusts or not, most of us sat up and played poker which was a big thrill when you were thirteen and a girl. So there we were, some of us smoking and all playing poker and feeling pretty big. It got towards two in the morning. Mrs. Parker had gone to bed. Suddenly spotlights from the road below came shooting up and a shaky police voice said, 'Come out or I'll fire!'

"We all punched Mrs. Parker and she got up painfully. She said, 'Oh, don't shoot, don't shoot, I'm coming down. I'm coming peacefully!

"She went down through the woods, half-dressed, and talked to them and quelled them. She told us when she came up, 'All right, don't anyone stand up. I told 'em I had a bunch of little babies up here!' "

She seemed truly to have a spell over the entire Cleveland Metropolitan Park Police Force. They seemed to sense the good in this woman and respond to it. They reacted to her innocence and simply sidestepped her mischief.

I remember her saying, "Okay, you can all stay overnight but I'm going to stay with the girls and we're going to sleep *here* and the boys will be over there—so!" So we were all there giggling and having an incredible time and who was trying to sleep? It was past midnight; finally the noise was too much for her. All of the sudden this spectre *leaped* out of the sleeping roll in her underwear—just underpants and brassiere—and *shouts us down!* We were stunned. Yet we thought what classic nerve to just stand there in underpants and brassiere!

We admired her all the more.

Once, one of Parker's friskier youngsters jumped her little horse over a fallen tree which proved too high for him, catching his hind legs. When he stopped, his fore feet were on the ground on the other side but his hind legs were up on the tree and the girl had catapulted over his head.

"I was too scared to turn around and look at the animal," she recalled. "I was on hands and knees. I looked up at Mrs. Parker to ask if my horse was dead or alive.

"She simply looked at me for a long moment—then she started to laugh. Everything was all right. As soon as she started laughing, I knew I could get up and that I could pull the horse out of the tree. But she really scared me that day because for a long moment, she didn't laugh.

"She stood silent as the tomb, allowing me to wonder."

"One year," said Jean Tomer, the day camp director, "I was thoroughly down and out at the end of camp and of course I *could* have gone up north to the cottage in Michigan. Adele said, 'Now, Jean, you're *going to go on this five-day ride!*'

"I said, 'Adele, I'm absolutely dead. In fifteen days I'm going to begin teaching school. I've got to get caught up.'

"*'I don't care what.'* she said. "There is Danny Boy and there's this cute little carriage. It has a trunk on the back. Get your bedroll and your clothes together—you won't have to do *one thing!'*

"And that's one time I didn't. This was one time I wasn't helping them pack, wasn't transporting any of her stuff. I said finally, 'Well, I give up. I just would *love* to go.' We were on the verge of leaving when a mother drove in the drive to leave her seven-year-old son for a week.

"Adele had said earlier, 'Anytime you want to, bring the little fellow out!'

"He showed up the morning we were departing for five days in the wilderness. The child went with us, of course. He was so tiny and cute and he rode in the covered wagon. We also rode in the hay wagon, he and I. It was a real entourage. Adele brought a buckboard and a summer canvas that you lay down on. We had a wonderful, wonderful time. At the CCC Camp, Jack, our colored cook (the Cream of Wheat boy) had all sorts of good food for us.

"Wild blackberries grew in abundance there and we gathered them, one and all, and then Jack made blackberry muffins. On all the roads running north and south we had

159

police escorts. This trip we were legitimate.

"When the little boy came home and went to school, the teacher asked him what he had done all summer. He said, 'I went West in a covered wagon!' It was the God's truth."

"The Thanksgiving ride?" the vet's wife laughed. Remember? Adele didn't go with us. Bob Gump was with us. Moose was along. Had we been riding with Mrs. Parker and we had come to an open expanse and were riding in a group, she would have said, 'All right, company by twos!' Well, God, you just did it! 'Company by fours!' You just did it. You didn't question.

"But she *wasn't* with us. We went down there. Bob was in the lead. He said, 'Let's GALLOP across!' Of course there was a police car and it spotted us. It started down the lane where the wood is. So, "Cheezit, the cops!' Off we went. We galloped across to Shepherd's Hill—*there's* a police car, too! Turn around! We flew back. The only place to go was on top of the hill. Up we go. We saw the police circle back.

"Bob said, quite dramatically, "that our only chance was to break up into groups of twos and just sort of amble back to the ranch. We did that and Moose got on the hill—Parker's Hill—and Moose went up to case the joint. In the meantime we had all pulled our coats inside out—or taken them off—so we wouldn't be recognized. Moose went up and we didn't hear a word, but we all were from Donofrio's Stables, we agreed, in case we got caught.

"Then Moose came down.

"Shhh! The cops are up there! The cops are up there!"

"Mrs. Parker answered their knock at the door. Well, of course it couldn't have been any of *her* people. They *knew* better than to try a fool stunt like that. The police drove out and Moose came and said, 'Okay, come on up!' We rushed up and got rid of the evidence just as the cruiser drove in again to see if any more horses had come in.

"We saw a group that sounded like the ones they described," we assured them. "They were from Donofrio's Stables."

"While us girls camped out," assured Shirley Harmon, "it wasn't unusual for boys at Parker's to sneak down and steal

160

our horses. Oh' we'd keep guard. We'd take turns. Mrs. Parker not only condoned such foolhardiness, she frequently planned it. One night one of the youngest girls claimed she saw a horse move but we figured she was seeing things. Suddenly off the horses flew. The boys messed up, but good. The bad thing was that they left the very heavy saddles. We were perhaps fourteen at the time.

"Then Mrs. Parker gathered us around her and she said, 'Well, we've got to have a pow-wow.' She elected five of us to go back and get those horses, and this was, perhaps, three o'clock in the morning, and we're just this high and we're down in the goddam dark Metropolitan Park sneaking around, scared to death, at least a couple miles back from the ranch.

"But we went back and, by gosh, we got 'em, and we snuck the mounts back down the cliff. Well, things like that! Who *else* would say, 'Go back and get 'em!' at that hour and under those circumstances? Mrs. Parker would.

"Of *course* you can't let the boys get the better of you!"

She might well have added, "And here is what you do to get rid of mosquitos. Now never forget this! You walk your horse around in a large circle for five or ten minutes. Then everybody run quickly toward the middle. You all should do this whenever you go down by the river across from Paradise. What keeps the mosquitos from following you into the center? They'll get confused. They'll keep following the circle."

On the three-day ride we would scout all kinds of tracks. "There goes raccoon tracks. There's a pile of deers'!" And she'd look at the tracks and tell us what the horse was doing—whether trotting or cantering and how long ago he had been there. She was superb at that. On one of the rides she carved her own trail through the timber. She simply chopped her way up this tall hill and all the way around to the far side to get to where we were going to make camp.

"But another time," a young woman added, "we were terribly lost in the middle of Metropolitan Park and ended up in Strongsville in the pitch dark. Somehow we missed our camper that was to have met us with food and warm clothing. I can recall having to tie our horses right next to us. We got practically no sleep, having ridden til after midnight. I remember Parker saying, 'Eat pancakes, they make you go to the bathroom in the morning.' I remember coming home and falling asleep on the floor and my mother trying to get me undressed and put to bed. I remember Mrs. Parker saying, 'Take your pants off in your sleeping bag so you don't get too hot. You'll be more comfortable.' She was seventy-five at the time.

"And I remember other times going down trail we had to turn right around cause she'd come across a lost dog or stray cat or a bird that had been hurt. We'd have to turn around and come back up so she could tend to it. And she'd point out—'See this beaver over here! See what it's doing? See that old barn owl?'

"We'd go down and chase our foxes. We saw one once. She said, 'Don't chase it! Don't chase it! It'll get away!' She adored them and used to bark at them. On overnights she'd say, 'I hear an owl!' and she'd hoot and it would hoot back, and she would run around trying to find the hooting owls."

Still another time, the usual campfire episodes were over and everyone was quieted down when the line of horses became untied from the tether rope, rousing everybody in camp. We all scurried into our clothes and grabbed flashlights as Mrs. Parker, in her longjohns, ran for the horses and hit a huge sewage puddle at least six feet across and filled to the brim. That put the can on the evening.

"Alexander's Crossing"... there was a fork in the bridle path coming in this direction towards the lake and there was a tree that had a big fork in it. There was a fallen log and there was a ritual there. She performed it every time we came there because the horse, Alexander, was buried there, and this was Alexander's Crossing.

Every time we rode by that spot... a little Indian something—that tree—nobody else had to perform it, but she always did. And how about Paradise? It's still there and still beautiful. One of the idyllic woodland glens.

She'd say, "Where do you want to ride to today?"

We'd say, "We want to go to Paradise."

"Her watchfulness for petting," laughed Sue Neneman Wendt, "was so typical of those outings, though in general the kids in that group very much grew up as brothers and sisters, and I kept in touch with many, many of them for years and years. By now they are scattered all over the world. We did everything together. Skating parties. Ranch parties. We horsed around together. We rode together. We took the horses down in the summer and rode bareback without shoes. We Indian-wrestled on horseback in the river and played a deadly capture-the-flag. These are very much part of. . . my fond memories. . ."

"Anything out of line," said the laundromat lady, "out you went! She was rough. Didn't believe in shenanigans. Many times when she had the whole gang out there—fellas in the barn, girls for the overnight. . . Mrs. Parker went scoutin' around the barns when they didn't know what she was doin'. She kept check. She kept very close check. Closer than they knew. Many times certain ones were forbidden on the overnights. She didn't tell 'em why but they *knew* why. My husband didn't like the idea of overnights for our daughter.

"I said, 'Frank, I've talked to that woman. I can't put it into words. I've never known anyone like her. . .' "

Adele Parker named every nook and corner in the valley, including trees and crossings: "The Galloping Grounds," "Happy Hunting Grounds," "Paradise," and "Paradise Lost." She adored making things secretive. Paradise was perfectly accessible by direct route. Oh, no! It had to be a secretive great adventure getting there. I am sure I have been places in that valley with Mrs. Parker that I will never find again.

She had a great big sense of fantasy which she could impart to others. When she took children riding, they would be Indian scouts, and all of the things which she had them do in the spirit of play-acting are the identical things that top trainers of the Olympic teams insist on, too—flexing in the saddle, crouching down on the side of your horse. . . all of these things, but she could make it into a great big exciting game.

When she died, her friend on the newspaper wrote:

"She rarely saw the inside of a church, yet she was a truly

religious person. Her temper for the out-of-doors, her creed, reverence for life, were all mixed with *mischief*. She was a genius with horses, completely understanding their psychology. But she was equally skilled with people, transforming many a youngster and morally supporting many of the world's wanderers.

"When she died, we still had so much to learn, so many questions to ask—not only about Buffalo Bill and circuses and vaudeville and above the ground airs with horses—but also about living.

"And... we will miss her."

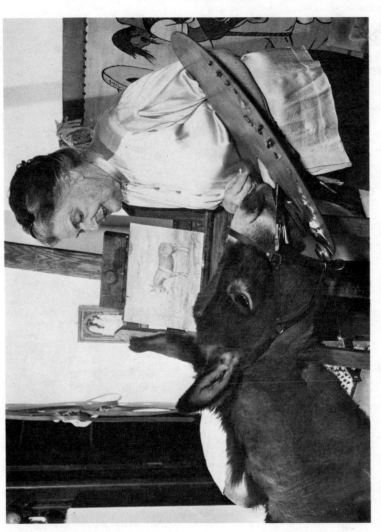

Mrs. Parker's famous kitchen served as hospital wing for sick chickens, goats and dogs—and also as an artist's studio. Critters of all sizes snooped and sniffed around the place as Mrs. Parker immortalized them on canvas.

If a horse had a tendency to rear or plunge, she would actually command him to do so. She would teach him to get *better* at it! Then she'd have him perform his acts of simple nasty behavior in the show ring and receive a thundering standing ovation from a crowd of impressed spectators.

CHAPTER 9

HORSES! HORSES! HORSES! HORSES!

We were on our way home, stopping off at Howard Johnson's, smelling of hay and manure. We had coffee and were getting ready to leave when Mrs. Parker, dressed in buckskins, came in with this dude. They had been to a performance of some sort and it turned out the fellow said he could sing like Gene Autry. He sounded more like our cat. I didn't fancy he could carry a tune in a bucket but he thought he could.

Anyway, the idea of a show came to her, with his help. He was going to star in the show and the horses would be incidental (the riders, too). Well, we're sitting around the table drinking coffee and the idea hatches. Mrs. Parker starts talking of how she could get the billboards—some of the things they had from the original Cody show, the original programs. . . and she'd take the music from each act just the way it had been played in the Buffalo Bill program.

"Pandemonium!" the neighbor squealed. "Complete and utter pandemonium! I can recall masses upon masses of horses, people, costumes, make-up—yelling, running, screaming—somehow it all jelled. I rode and shot bow and arrow. This was part of our training—'Just hold on with your legs and thighs, dear. . .' I was so determined I was going to please her! It really wasn't a professional show. It was more like, 'Here we are. We're having fun. We can do something that's worth watching. If you care to watch, fine. If you don't, good-bye. This is what we do, and we're having a marvelous time!'"

"From an average citizen's point of view," sighed another, "it occasionally got tedious. I'm sure Mrs. Parker sensed this and so she passed out Wild West show tickets up and down the street. Since you had to put up with the noise anyway, you could at least come over and see what was going on. I figured I could stand banging and shooting for two days, matinee and evening."

"Oh, we had real Indians," said the lady in charge of make-up. "And we had a few scouts painted up to take the part. Of course we couldn't have genuine train robbers released from jail to take part in the show. She probably never thought of that... *Everything* happened at Parker's Ranch. You just went in there and you said to yourself, 'I never thought it would happen,' but everything happened.'"

I've seen Mrs. Parker ride proudly in her own show—and get tossed right on her very substantial backside—come down with a crack you could hear across the ring. She would get up with absolutely no embarrassment, saying, "Well, that's one way to cure a charley horse!"

But her shows were always lengthy. I suppose when you were a child they didn't seem so endless. They also were very hot and dirty.

"I had just gotten to the gate when somebody said Mrs. Parker's horse was shot," the ticket-taker said. "'Somebody fired from the audience!' they said again and again. I could see Winch was hit and I saw them leading him off while Mrs. Parker was being attended to, having been dumped and shaken up. She said, 'I'm all right. Somebody take care of Winch!' That's what I did. In a moment Eugenia was applying ice packs and I rushed into the house to get a fresh batch. Then Dr. Hagarty got there and he started helping out. And I felt sorry for him. I work for the VA and he had been a resident there in neurosurgery. He was a good neuro-surgeon, very highly respected. So this woman comes up to him and asks, 'Is this the horse that got shot?'

"Yes."

"Are you the vet?"

"No, I'm a neuro-surgeon."

"She went away, thinking he was sure some smart-ass vet."

One rider recalled an authentic Blackfoot Indian. *"Was he ever good!* He might still be in town. I don't think he was one who went back to the reservation. He'd scalp a fellow who had tomato catsup under a wig. Then a war whoop—oh, boy! This was impressive at night because they'd turn the lights down and everybody'd hightail it in the dark.

"Who else," she asked, "would drive a station wagon full of Indians from North Olmsted downtown and have to listen to them practice war whoops? Practiced all the way there and all the way home. They'd come early Sunday morning for rehearsal and would chant all day long. They drove the goddam neighbors mad."

"She fell off Winchester," said a friend, "right down next to the American Legion train. Winch roared by and they were shooting blanks. One was too close. Winch went right up against a fence, shied away and she tumbled off on her head. I stood with my mouth open, it all happened so fast. Then Winch went into one of his nervous breakdowns from that. But she got up—shook it off. She was 75 years old and dazed, and went on. She said, 'I'm all right, get ready for the next act.'"

"We used to go out there and sit in that little dining area off the kitchen," smiled the promoter. *Always* a coffee pot on and a big fat kiss when you went in. *So* gracious! The Wild West Show started with our getting together talkin' about the show for Mother's Day. Of course there'd be scads of her pupils in the new extravaganza and others who had horses out there. A few acts came in from out of town, bringing their mounts with them. Mrs. Parker could handle a 45 and had a beautiful riding horse and wore a stately hat and her hair tied in a ribbon.

"A series of acts was decided. One was robbing the train (she would be the robber). She conjured up a script whereby she'd fall off a horse while someone chased her—the train crew, I guess. She'd pretend she was shot, spring from her animal and get up like this—ugh! as though marshalling her last ounce of strength—BANG! went that goddam 45!"

News writer Jan Mellow of the Cleveland *Plain Dealer* once had to hit the dirt along with the rest of us. The Indians were coming and if you didn't go down, Parker knocked you down. When those Indians rode for your head, you dropped to all fours. . .

Did interest in the show die? Oh, yes. Oh, Yes. It was run to the ground. The first show, of course, was for the crippled children—the finest year. The next year or so, the Kiwanis.

169

Then nobody. And it got poorer and poorer as it went on. It just was not part of her comprehension that it is possible to run a good thing to death.

As for rehearsals, you never knew what was going to happen. For the thing you rehearsed the day before never was the same the following day. Everything had to be done bing-bing-bing—with 75 people. You don't get organized like that. I had my own horse, my own costume, I was an Arab or something. Really, nobody knew what they were doing. The day of the performance it was a bloody miracle she didn't have a stroke—or that *we* didn't.

Everything was completely changed from the night before. At one rehearsal a horse died and we had to carry him off. We didn't have a team and the show was starting the next day. It was typical. It was the showman. And of course none of us were professionals. Any sign of panic antagonized her. We all would come through, of course, and, at the end, she had nothing but praise for everybody. She was like the storm on Bald Mountain giving way to the serene dawn.

She had all of the horses galloping about the ring, running around, no one holding them, and thirty people lying on the ground out there... And how could they have such *faith?* Why weren't they *panic-stricken?* Because Mrs. Parker had said, "Now a horse won't step on ya, he'll step over ya." My God, I don't know! But nothing bad *did* happen. It all tied together beautifully. For when the moment of truth arrived, this is what you did for Parker. No one was paid. They did it for *her.* Those girls hung upside down doing the "death-drag"—they could have been killed... the covered wagon burning... the band playing... one never knew what those horses might do with all that racket... screaming Indians. Everybody. Every year. We did it for Parker.

"One year," a discouraged girl said, "we had the Traveling Troubadour—Andy something-or-other. He didn't know how to ride. They were playing 'Home On The Range' and he was singing, 'Oh, Bury Me Not On The Lone Prairie-e-e!' Big deal!"

"No, that's not the way we did it in the show!" Adele would holler. She'd charge out there screaming.

"But when the day came and they charged in with those

170

flags flying," recalled a rider, "I nearly cried. When the music started, your nerves—you were just so worn out rehearsing. She had tried to get her ideas across to you... and with the real Indians there and her war whoop and the rehearsals and the tom-toms and the Indian dances—well, you don't see any of that on Euclid Avenue..."

News Report
"At the rehearsal Friday, a horse fell dead of a heart attack. That Mrs. Parker was shaken by the fall was made apparent, but later she did not know quite what had happened. Her horse was cut on the right flank, perhaps by her spur as she went over. His place for the remainder of the show was taken by Traveler, who seemed to do equally as good a job. The only hurt Mrs. P. would acknowledge was her disappointment that the show she and her pupils had worked so hard on for two months was marred by the accident. 'It just made it a little more real,' she said later. 'The script called for me to die in the train robbery, anyway...' "

"Her old draft horse had died," said Jean McKenna, "one of the team that used to pull the hayride wagon. It died and she buried it, but not deep enough. The Health Department was out there and got chains and started pulling it out. Oh, God, did she put up a stink! See, once you're buried, you're buried to *rest!* Horse or no horse, you *rest!*

"I went back there once. There were little indentations in the ground and one of them had a horse head in the clay and then these two big stones. I asked around. I said, 'Is that a grave?' The man who took care of the horses said, 'No—just a little artwork.' I said, 'No, there are three in a row. They're graves. You can tell me or not, but they are.' "

"It's Hard to Believe Charles is Gone"
(Cleveland Plain Dealer)
"North Olmsted police yesterday finally disposed of Charles, a horse belonging to colorful Adele von Ohl Parker. Mrs. Mary Alice Lynch, an attractive member of City Council, heaved a sigh of relief last night. She told council that numerous residents on Mastick Road in her ward had complained about the smell coming from Parker's Ranch.

"Charles, a member of the covered wagon team, died last Friday—one of Adele's best-loved horses who was scheduled to cavort in her Buffalo Bill Wild West Show benefit last week-end.

"Mrs. Parker claimed that she tried but was unable to dispose of Charles so she called police yesterday morning. Mrs. Lynch, under mounting pressure, proposed that legislation be drafted making it mandatory for owners of dead animals to dispose of them. Solicitor Clarence J. Oviatt said it was not the municipality's responsibility."

"Well," the trainer said, "if the animal dies and the blood can be drained properly within a certain length of time, then the meat is useable for foxfood or dogfood, but if not, it isn't good to use. If it isn't drained right at the proper time, none of these boys want to touch it. Then you got to get somebody who'll dig a hole or who'll haul it away—or SOMETHING! You really have to have one of those front-end loaders or a scoop shovel to bury a horse today. It's a mess, particularly in winter. I took my horse to the zoo and had it shot.

"The real trouble," the trainer insisted, "is that we're reliant upon wells. You don't bury a horse too close to a well. Where to bury a horse so it doesn't contaminate the underground water supply is a problem. Council runs and hides. . . they don't even want a say about it. They say 'do something,' but they won't say what you can do. You can't put 'em above the ground. You can't put 'em below the ground. In Parker's case, she had horse on top of horse back there."

"The whole story about Charley," explained the vet, "was that Cleveland Clinic wanted blood from a horse. I called Parker's and asked if they had a horse I could bleed and that the clinic would pay them $25.00. 'Yes,' she said. I went out and did it."

A performer recalled the horse's death.

"Even while the horse was being prepared, Mrs. Parker was in tears. Somehow I think she thought of herself as Judas with her thirty pieces of silver, and Christ in the form of old Charley was being hoisted up in a tree above old Chester's grave. They cut his neck and we all stood there. It was sheer torture for Mrs. Parker. They just hoisted him up. She told them how to do it but of course they did it their way. After they let him down, he was charging people and was nasty.

"All I can remember," a guest confirmed, "is Charley dropping over. A very sad situation. She ran over to Charley, put his head in her lap and cried, 'Don't leave me now!' That's when everybody started gathering around. 'Where are you going!' she hissed. She put a cover over Charley and we returned to the ring. Later she said, 'Charley would have wanted it that way.' "

The Department of the Interior spokesman explained about the Indians in her shows:

"The American Indians who appeared in Mrs. Parker's shows volunteered their services through the North American Committee of Cleveland, Incorporated," he said, "whose officers are members of the Mohave, Sioux, Apache, Shishone and Oneida tribes. The organization was established in Cleveland in the 50's to help Indian people in that city better meet some of the adjustment problems of living in an urban community, and to help preserve Indian culture and heritage. I do not believe the story of their attempt to burn down Mrs. Parker's house after absconding with her wine," he added. "Well, not in every detail. . ."

She had arranged a press party to give the lowdown on the wild west show. She had a chuckwagon and first handed out broiled steaks but no knives or forks. The people from the media had to tear loaves of bread apart and make man-sized sandwiches. "It was," she made clear, "the way we did it in the West." Then she served coffee which she guaranteed was simmered with a stick in it.

"No," the caller said, "the people in the saddle horse business wouldn't attend her doin's. It was all western stuff, all wild west stuff. English people don't go for that, now that's the truth. She was pure circus person to them, all the way through."

"What did I *enjoy* about her shows?" asked the man selling brushes. "*Her*. She, Herself. Her sportsmanship. The way she acted. She was magnificent. All the other ones never showed up like she done. . ."

"I remember during the rehearsal," said the Arabian rider, "everything was going wrong. First the show was on, then it

173

was off. For an hour and a half, this went on. Every time you got your horse out, the show was off. You put it away. Somebody'd storm by and say, 'The show's back on again.' I'd saddle him up again. About the sixth time that happened, I was ready to put him away and leave him away. They finally put the show on that night. People sat out there in the rain and watched it. And once there was a hurt Indian. It took a month of Sundays to get there with the ambulance. Uncle Frank and I jumped over the fence and helped everybody look at him."

"I was making a delivery in a bar," said the Budweiser man, "Someone looks at the TV and says, 'Oh, boy, cowboys!' I look up and I say, 'Hey, that's my kid!' And the bartender says, 'Where is he—out west at a rodeo?' And I says, 'No, Parker's Ranch!' He nearly fell off the stool."

"What Dad saw on the bar television," explained Marty Harayda, "was the TV preview of the 1959 Parker's Ranch Wild West Show. It was a scene where Ron Schmidtke and me held up the train and stole all the mailbags. I chased him around, caught up with him, got in a fight—really the best fight we ever had. We couldn't rehearse it. It just felt good. It felt realistic. I wish I could have seen it, myself.

"Everything seemed to go smoothly. Ron jumped at me. I was just getting up on one knee and as he came through the air I caught him by the belt and flipped him—he did a somersault and landed in a heap. I raced over and took a poke at him just as he was getting up and of course he just flipped over backwards. The televised rehearsal was more for advertising than anything else 'cause that was the year for the crippled children.

"Parker was real proud of that show. I'd rope a kid. He was another villain. I'd run as fast as that darn horse would go around the ring with this kid dangling at the end like a carrot. He just flopped end over end as the TV cameras kept going. Of course we had a mountain of clothes on. I shouted, 'What are we going to do with him and everybody yells, 'Hang him! Hang him! Blast him!' and I took a gun and emptied it into him and, of course, he jumped every time a bullet struck him. We saw the movies later. Maybe a little hammy, but fast-moving, anyway. It was kind of dangerous in a way..."

Who could forget the year they tried to ignite the wagon with water and put it out with gasoline! You can't blame owners of thoroughbred horses for not subjecting their steeds to such madness. They sometimes just explode in madness like that was. I am sure I shall always remember the burning canvas falling in hot pieces on all of us when the moment came to run for our horses. You simply fled through the mob of animals, hoping to find your own. That night she told the fellow, "Now the wind is blowing from the east. You be sure to put the wagon like *this* so the canvas won't blow into the arena!" Of course he didn't listen. Man!

"I am directly behind the wagon," said the Chippewa rider—the scene where the wagon is fired, you know? A flaming arrow shot into it. So the thing goes up like the Chicago fire. They unhitched the team and the team's standing over at the side and I'm hiding there, standing far clear of the exploding guns.

"Then Charley drops dead—right on my ankle. And what are you going to do with Charley? Somebody calls up. But all next day and the day after that, nobody comes. It's August and Charley's lying out there, parboiling. Someone threw a tarp over him, and that made it worse.

"Finally they dug a hole and saturated it with lime and just chucked him in. But then somebody put that tarp that had been over Charley all those days on the fence going into the orchard. I remember the newspaper headlines: "Must Charley Smell Up Our Neighborhood?" Another: "Charley Is Stinking Up North Olmsted!" Poor old Charley. Just a horse but he had the last smell."

"I counted them—1600 more gray hairs a performance!" said one mother. Said another, "I disappointed her so and the fact just crushed me. She insisted that I be one of the old western women and my boy Jimmy would be my son. We were to hide behind the covered wagon before it burnt to the ground. I just couldn't go *that* far..."

The covered wagon would enter usually as a two-horse hitch. One year they did substitute a pair of bewildered oxen. The settlers would come in, make camp and light a fire. As they said their evening prayer, Indians pounced from everywhere, firing the wagon. Well, the damn thing either didn't start or everything burned around our heads. Sometimes they had to pour kerosene on the spot where the arrow was to go through and Bob Gump had to run up with his cigarette lighter and splatter the canvas top. I usually exited with my horse at that point and plenty of others were right behind me!

OFFICER'S REPORT
(North Olmsted Police Department)

"While on routine patrol I was sent to Parker's Ranch to investigate someone shooting live ammunition. When I arrived at Parker's there was a wild west show in progress. I talked to Mrs. Parker and asked her if she had any knowledge of anyone using live ammunition and she said only one boy was using it in his act.

"She then called Mr. Matthews over and at this time I advised them of the ordnance prohibiting discharging of firearms in the city, but that by order of the chief they could use blank ammunition.

"They both agreed. I then asked Mr. Matthews to see the revolver which he used in the act and asked how it was used. He explained and I again advised him against using live ammunition and asked him if he remembered shooting directly at any people. He said he had missed two balloon targets on the way down and that he had attempted to break them on his way out of the ring. On Mr. Matthews' exit from the ring he would have had to be shooting directly into the spectators.

"Some minutes after the fact, three female spectators noticed blood on their clothing."

"No sir, I didn't go to her shows," the man across the street said. "Saturdays and Sundays are our busy days here. But I heard the goings on from here. I seen some of the wagons over the car roofs. I heard the noise, the commotion, the pistol shots. It looked like it were all there. She packed 'em in. She was a master at that. Nobody can do it again. Nobody will have the know-how, now. She was the last and they're all gone, now. Most folks who knew her have even moved away."

Now there were lots of people donating money and time to the first wild west show. Promotion was first class. Seemingly from nowhere sprang new lights around the ring, a new corral, new fences... Of course Mrs. Parker never let a good thing die, either. The first show was fine—a great success. The second one was a little sticky and didn't quite get the rally. By the time she had the third one, they said, "Good God, not again!' From there on it was all down hill. The columnists tried their best to rally with her: "The favorite old acts will again be presented this year. . ." The wild west shows died on the vine.

When troubles leaped out from nowhere, however, Adele Parker never winced. When the target-shooting went amiss and some of the shot went into the crowd, Parker never lost her poise, even when the girls found themselves pelted with blood. Here was Adele sitting over by the barn with all these policemen. She took the act out of the show the next day—reluctantly. . .

"I was out there in the front pasture *stuck*," the banker said, "so I called the Auto Club and Bakers came over. He couldn't get the truck up close enough and when he did put a cable on it, his wheels only spun and broke my tail light trying to push me. Mrs. Parker announced over the loud speaker, 'HEY, SOME OF YOU HUSKY MEN GET ON OVER THERE AND GIVE THAT FELLA A HAND! That was the end of it. Five guys showed up and I got out."

"Then," said the early pioneer woman, "the Indians suddenly shot the wagon and it started burning and they swarmed in from the corners and butchered everybody and you just fell down and lay there. Of course the horses got all excited and they would just start running and you tried your best to lie in a group. In fact I would try to fall down by the steers for shelter but my husband always wanted to do a little fighting before he died. . ."

"I had never done it before!" swore 50-year-old Russ Janus. "I never have since. I grabbed the horn, hit my feet and flew up in the saddle. Everybody said, 'Gee, I didn't know you could do that!' I didn't either, but I couldn't see standing

177

around in such traffic!"

One woman rode on the front of the wagon with the fella who led the team in.

"I said, 'Hey, anybody ridin' with you?' He said, 'Yeah, YOU!' So I got up front and rode into the arena as kind of the old mother goin' west in the long dress and petticoat bit. Then he stopped and hopped off and held the team. Well, a stagecoach is higher than you think. I jumped down onto the first step—a great big knuckly-like thing—the wheel hub——and when I stepped down from that, my skirt hooked and I went upside down with my feet in the air. The fella took it all in, enjoying himself, then just flipped my skirt over and I slumped in a heap.

"Later my husband asked, 'You have your bikini panties on?'

"No! I had on the red ones from Pennys!"

"He said, 'Gee, I thought you'd been scalped."

"We were supposed to ride Roosevelt and Wilkie, two little mistreated mules," the pretty girl said. "Roosevelt was a sweetie but Wilkie was a bastard. They knew how to step up on the platform and do a few cute tricks and amuse people. So we dressed up like tramps, my friend and I. It was a rotten, muddy, ugly day and the mules took the time to roll in some ooze by the main gate. I saw that I was at Wilkie's shoulder like I was told to be, and was about to mount.

"No problem. Only I didn't stay with the shoulders. He backed up and sat down. Before I knew it, up came those feet. I knew just for a split second—for I recall the flashing hooves—that my face would be smashed. But all he did was take half a tooth. He grazed the nose and the cheek and the mouth. Since then the roots of several teeth have died and we've had endless root canal work done.

"That's my memory of the wild west show."

But the producer, director and principal player of any Parker's Ranch extravaganza was Adele Parker, herself. Her yell was something between a banchee and a whoopee. After all the wild west shows she'd mount Traveler, rear up in the air, and give that wild yell as she tore out. She was *always* doing that. We used to make bets that she'd die on a horse—no matter how old she was, or how sick.

178

A rare photograph from the 1907 Buffalo Bill Wild West Show captures Adele Parker leaping from original Overland Stage with pistol in hand. She pleaded for as much action as Colonel Cody would allow but confessed having problems with Indians who kept forgetting it was a game.

Adele believed in very little, intellectually. She loved to get a group of priests out on the trail at sunup, gaze across the chasm and say to them, "The *world* is my cathedral—this valley is my church!" She was not sure there is a God, yet she always bent in a spiritual direction.

CHAPTER 10

FAREWELL AND FAREWELL

It did look as if Mrs. Parker would never die. So much so that when she did, finally, no one believed it. They don't really believe it yet.

"Mrs. Parker," said her friend Sue Wendt, "would not sell her old cars while she lived. This, like so many things was left for someone else to do. Eugenia had to take the horses down and have them destroyed. She had to take little Hammy and Mrs. Parker's Traveler and my heart ached when she stopped in here in tears."

Persons who had not been near the ranch in twenty years called after the funeral, saying, "Do you need $3,000? Do you need $4,000? Do you need $5,000 to keep the place going in her memory? They didn't want it to die. No one knew these people even cared about her. Or would have guessed. But Mrs. Parker told us kids I don't know how many times, "You understand that when I die, there will be no more Parker's Ranch."

She said once, "I hope that when I die they take me down in the valley and throw an old saddle blanket over me." That's all she said on the subject then. And all she ever said.

"Even at the funeral," whispered a disciple, "she had the expression of a little girl. I recall those last times she was teaching fine points, it was the same—not childishness—but like your boss who is either an executive or a little boy, with hardly any middle ground."

Details of the burial were private. And unknown. Nobody really knows. There were stories of scattering her ashes free over the valley and the lake of the estate where she was born. No one who had known her would have thought it inappropriate. The ashes of Jack, one of the ranch men, are part of the valley. She waited and waited for the proper day, the proper wind—so he could be where he wanted to be. For a long time the ashes of Percy and Winnona hung around in jars waiting for the trip to New Jersey. Us kids found them, snooping around. We did a lot of snooping around.

"I don't like to look at dead people," the trainer said. "Especially Mrs. Parker. I remember her saying once she was like a horse. Most horses, if you go into the barn at night and they are lying down, they'll get up as soon as you enter. She felt they never liked to be seen lying down. It was private... and you never—or seldom—saw *her* lying down, either."

Asked about a duck or a chicken she would say, "Well, it's been so long since I was one, I don't know." Or, "When I was a duck or a chicken, I did this... it's been so long since I was a goat..."

"It was Jimmy's first experience in a funeral parlor," the mother said. "The first dead body he'd seen. We did take him. He wanted to go desperately. Of course they had her in full riding regalia which I thought was marvelous because I couldn't imagine her any other way. The huge horseshoe... her riding crop in her hand..."

The children took it very, very hard. They kept calling one another up and resurrecting it over and over again and virtually gushed warm tears over the telephone.

"I wouldn't have missed it," the trainer said. "I went to find out all the dirt about what was going to happen to the place. I didn't want to miss out on *anything*... I wanted to see all the people I hadn't seen for a hundred years. Everybody was there...

"Everybody!"

In her casket she wore frilly lace at the wrist, light blue string tie, white blouse with lace. There was a horseshoe wreath made of green and white carnations. Beautiful. Appropriate. Who will see that again in a lifetime?

She rode, they say, the day she died. That night she bathed a duck which was to appear on the Mike Douglas show the following day. The duck had been hurt and to keep it away from the other ducks, she had put him in the coal bin, after which he had to be bathed and dried. She suffered a heart attack and died in the early hours of the following morning.

She would say, "Oh, just take my ashes for a ride in the

valley." It sounded like such a sweet idea when she said it. I hope they *did* scatter her over the park. I'm enough of a Parker's Rancher to approve of it—my God, she *belongs* to that valley!

"There was always much secrecy about the ranch," the trick rider said. "We always said, 'Once Mrs. Parker is gone, the ranch will die, too, because nobody who remains there would want it. It was true. Who wants to live in a haunted house?"

"She said something very interesting about two weeks before she died," a friend recalled. "She looked at me and put her arm around me and said, 'You know, honey, I have hated this place like poison for twenty-nine years—and all of the sudden I'm finding I'm loving it." She said, "Now you watch. When you start to love something, that's the time you have to leave it."

And when the child heard Mrs. Parker was dead, she did not go on to the schoolroom. She set out to walk the two miles into the valley to tell the foxes. She would go down and tell the foxes. The foxes would wish to know.

Wrote Harold Van Schaack, of Columbus, Ohio, an old friend, "The accounts of the passing of Mrs. Adele von Ohl Parker stated accurately and necessarily, it is assumed, that 'there were no immediate survivors.' Such an obituary always increases the essential sadness in the death of anyone, but surely in the case of Mrs. Parker, there is singular mitigation.

"Here was a lady who left unnumbered men, women, and particularly children sensing a truly personal loss scattered in areas and diverse in status beyond any possibility of identification or estimate.

"Fortune smiled kindly on the community and especially on North Olmsted, Ohio, the day Mrs. Parker settled down on Mastick Road to spend nearly four decades in ornamenting and serving a locality which she came to love and which may never have appreciated her enough. Her disregard of superficial, passing convention so closely worshipped by lesser folk was exceeded only by her consistent adherence to life's eternal verities. Her charm, her witty intelligence, her industry, her charity, her loyalty to man and beast alike, made for a way of life magnificent to observe and a privilege to sometimes share.

"For one of a later generation to drop around and spend time with this fascinating character was to convince the visitor that he had in fact at least a small part of an enchanting past which he had, up till that time, supposed he had entirely missed.

"Her teaching of the young—not only of horsemanship but of life itself can only be described as a grand continuing performance... To have crossed the pathway of Mrs. Parker was one of life's rare dividends for all who now mourn... an uncommon lady."

At the funeral were the fanciest costumes. People who could barely get there in beaten down farm trucks came. They all loved her one way or another. They cared. It seemed that anybody who had run into her somewhere along the line felt an obligation to see that she was taken care of. When her debts got too heavy, these same friends got up some publicity and had nice $25 a plate dinners and other events. And this would float them for awhile.

Then she'd get everybody steaming mad by going out and buying some new horses which they could not afford and had no room for and couldn't feed. But she'd do it—and then they would be without money again.

We were jammed into the funeral parlor like horses—in every direction. Fortunately where we were seated, we could see the minister in front of the casket. Out on the black-topped parking lot were the jalopies and the farm trucks and the Cadillacs.

"It was the most amazing thing," said news writer Hulda Lesher. "In this day of youth taking the rap for all of our international nastiness and evil, Ma'am's funeral visitors were 95% young. Teen-agers. Well-behaved. Dressed to the teeth. It gave me a great feeling of comfort, of satisfaction for this country. Many would have taken bets—eight to one, twenty to one—that they would have come in dungarees and sweatshirts, if at all. No, sir. Not a one.

"And you had the feeling Mrs. Parker was somehow con-

184

scious of it all. That she was enjoying every single moment of it. You had the most curiously strong sensation that the pixie was still around."

At the auction, for five dollars you could acquire a fringe jacket, boots, chaps, or a long flowing dress full of memories and ghosts.

"We simply wanted a memento," somebody said. "We bought a red tack chest. Also a sidesaddle for two or three dollars. And the little picture. Someone in the house sold us that. A few sketches. A shoetree for the top of a boot that she had. I bought a lot of britches but threw 'em out because they really weren't good. There was one cute bolero with lots and lots of fringe on it—the whole mess cost so little. . . five dollars tops. Why, the *bolero* was worth that. . ."

"It was like a whole era passing," the girl cried. "Part of my childhood tearing to shreds."

"Did you catch the labels on the theater trunks tossed out in the yard by the auction people? Heidelberg Grand Hotel. . . Hotel du lac Lucerne. . . Marseille Splendide Hotel. . . Hotel Richmond Geneve. . . Hotel Regina Venise. . . *Jesus!*"

Many of the show costumes were authentic. All the Indian stuff was. Beautiful Indian headdresses. Did you ever see such things? Brand new picture frames never out of the wrappings. I went out Sunday to pick up the bench and I found this old sewing machine from the front room. Someone had said to her, "Adele, can you use this?"

"Yes, I'll take it and learn to sew!"

Everybody knew she wouldn't, but the *notion* was the joy of it. . . All of those rusted falling down chariots—all of that stuff in the upper barn—all of those old horse collars. Who would *use* those things?

Young people swarmed the place seeking "simply anything" that belonged to her. Just to have it. A spoon. A ribbon. A piece of string. . .

"This knife was hers," a young man said. "Don't ask me where she got it. But look at its age and condition. The intricacy. I don't know the story of it. You never knew who gave it to her. What she used it for. What show it was in.

But it was her knife. . ."

One of the absent could not condone it.

"This sort of thing I cannot—I *will* not—go to see. I think of the beautiful things I knew about her. But this is—*scavaging!* Not interested, thank you. Scavaging a piece of a person's life! I like to remember the *wholeness* of her. Boxes of her fringed jackets and costumes for five dollars a box! That's so sad. I don't know how else you dispose of them, but to me it's ludicrous! It's exhibiting her life in bits and pieces and dispersing them to the highest bidder. . ."

"After her death," said the neighbor Jean McKenna, "we had to close the gate back there. People would drive in or drive by slow. . . curious. . . drive around and stop—and look.

"What are you going to do? Tear it down? Build a monument and have Sunday visitors? How about a public picnic grounds?"

"My God!"

"It's funny," she said. "People ask, 'Where do you live?'

"Oh, we live next to Parker's Ranch."

"It's a landmark, you know? Long after the funeral, people still came, not knowing of her death—people from Maryland, Virginia, Oklahoma. They came up here, and they still come. I met a man—I can't remember his name—who performed with the circus all these years, and had performed with Mrs. Parker. He'd retired from the circus, so he thought he would come up and say hello.

"He looked like one of those old fellows who was married to long distance and he had stuff he wanted to show her and give to her. I had to break the news to him. God, the tears rolled down his face. I felt so sorry 'cause he'd been all over—*everywhere*—and he'd never forgot her.

"A policeman came down here last summer and he just sat in the driveway back here and I went back and asked him if he were looking for someone or if I could help him. He just said, 'You know, I remember this place as a kid,' and he went on and on, going over it all in his mind. He said, 'You know, North Olmsted has lost something. . . it was a big thing here when she used to have those shows. North Olmsted then was *someplace!* Nobody ever heard of North Olmsted, Ohio—except being the place where Parker's Ranch was. . ."

"Therefore. . . take no thought. . ."

Therefore I say unto you, Take no thought for your life, what ye shall eat, or what ye shall drink; and yet for your body, what ye shall put on. Is not the life more than meat, and the body more than raiment?

Behold the fowls of the air; for they sow not, neither do they reap, nor gather into barns; yet your heavenly Father feedeth them. Are ye not much better than they?

Which of you by taking thought can add one cubit unto his stature?

And why take ye thought for raiment? Consider the lilies of the field, how they grow; they toil not, neither do they spin. . .

Wherefore, if God so clothe the grass of the field, which today is, and tomorrow is cast into the oven, shall he not much more cloth you, O ye of little faith?

There take no thought, saying, What shall we eat? or, What shall we drink? or, Wherewithal shall we be clothed? For your heavenly Father knoweth that ye have need of all these things.

But seek ye first the kingdom of God, and his righteousness; and all these things shall be added unto you.

Take therefore no thought for the morrow; for the morrow shall take thought for the things of itself. Sufficient unto the day is the evil thereof.

The Holy Bible

The Indians' Twenty-Third Psalm

The Great White Father above us is a great Chief. I am His and with Him I want not. He throws me a rope, and the name of the rope is love; and He draws me to Him. And he draws me where the grass is green, and the water is good, and I eat and lie down satisfied.

Sometime, it may be very soon, it may be longer, it may be a long, long time, He will draw me into a place between mountains. It is dark there, but I will not draw back, I'll not be afraid, for it is there between these mountains that the Chief Shepherd will meet me.

Sometimes He makes the love rope into a whip, but afterwards He gives me a staff to lean on. He spreads before me a table with all kinds of food, and His hand rests upon my head, and all the tiredness is gone. My cup He fills until it runs over.

What I tell you is true, I lie not, for this trail that is way ahead will stay with me all through life, and afterwards I will go to live in the Big Teepee and sit down by the Shepherd Chief forever.

Her ideal and champion nearly all of her life, Buffalo Bill became a household word with all who rode with Mrs. Parker. At the end of her life, her dream was to raise money to purchase statues of "the Colonel" for every school in the country.